Everyday
GLUTEN~FREE
SLOW COOKING

Everyday
GLUTEN~FREE
SLOW COOKING

**140
Easy &
Delicious
Recipes**

Kimberly Mayone
and Kitty Broihier, MS, RD

STERLING
New York

STERLING
New York

An Imprint of Sterling Publishing
387 Park Avenue South
New York, NY 10016

STERLING and the distinctive Sterling logo are registered trademarks of
Sterling Publishing Co., Inc.

© 2012 by Kimberly Mayone and Kitty Broihier, MS, RD

ISBN 978-1-4027-8553-5 (hardcover)
ISBN 978-1-4027-8945-8 (ebook)

Distributed in Canada by Sterling Publishing
c/o Canadian Manda Group, 165 Dufferin Street
Toronto, Ontario, Canada M6K 3H6
Distributed in the United Kingdom by GMC Distribution Services
Castle Place, 166 High Street, Lewes, East Sussex, England BN7 1XU
Distributed in Australia by Capricorn Link (Australia) Pty. Ltd.
P.O. Box 704, Windsor, NSW 2756, Australia

A Buoy Point Media Production
Interior Design: Fabia Wargin
Drawings: Amelia Leon

For information about custom editions, special sales, and premium
and corporate purchases, please contact Sterling Special Sales
at 800-805-5489 or specialsales@sterlingpublishing.com.

Manufactured in the United States of America

2 4 6 8 10 9 7 5 3 1

www.sterlingpublishing.com

To my parents, Harry and Patricia Sundik,
for your love, support, babysitting, and appetites.

— KIMBERLY MAYONE

To my children, Jack and Amelia,
with never-ending love,
and in memory of my father, whom I miss every day.

— KITTY BROIHIER

Acknowledgements

We have written three books together and it still humbles us to see how many people actually help us deliver a cookbook. First, we would like to thank our agent, Lisa Ekus-Saffer, and her daughter, Sally Ekus, for seeing the value of this project and finding a great home for this book at Sterling Publishing. Jennifer Williams, our editor at Sterling, not only took a personal interest in this book (even going so far as to test some of the initial recipes on her teenage son), but was a delight to work with and made our jobs as authors incredibly easy. Thanks also to our very talented photographer friend Kevin Keith, whose photos of our food are true works of art, and to Sterling art director Elizabeth Mihaltse, who designed the book cover with such a fresh, inviting, and appealing style. Thanks, too, to designer Fabia Wargin for the beautiful layout of this book.

We would be remiss if we didn't thank the many people in our lives who have supported us in this endeavor. Mark Mayone, cookbook husband extraordinaire, made countless grocery store runs and regularly shuttled recipe samples between our homes. Great big thanks go to our families, who happily ate one slow-cooked meal after another for many months during the writing of this book. We would also like to thank our friends and neighbors who taste-tested, watched our kids so we could work, and cheered us on to the finish line. Last but not least, we are grateful to our new friend, Melissa Coriaty at Verbena, our favorite South Portland café, who kept us fueled with coffee and yummy food during our weekly editorial meetings at her shop.

Contents

Foreword

It is very safe to say that we are fond of our slow cookers. Even when we are not writing slow cooker cookbooks, we use them all year-round, pretty much every week. When Kimberly's husband began tinkering with a gluten-free diet at home, she approached it with a positive attitude and looked to all the foods he could eat, rather than at the foods he would have to restrict. And as the primary cook at casa Mayone, Kimberly strove to blend gluten-free dishes with her own style of cooking in such a way that the whole family could enjoy their meals without feeling that they were on a "special diet." Kitty helped out when it came time to navigate condiments and other ingredients that might or might not contain gluten. Somewhere along the line, after some coffee and conversation, it seemed reasonable to start compiling gluten-free slow cooker recipes into a book.

It made good sense for us to approach this project the same way we approached our first slow cooker book, *The Everyday Low-Carb Slow Cooker Cookbook* (DeCapo Press, 2004). Our recipes are geared to folks who want budget-friendly, flavorful meals that require little effort. We recognize that eating gluten-free can be a challenge in itself. We also respect the original intent of the slow cooker—to simplify cooking. So whether you are new to gluten-free cooking or new to slow cooking or not new to either of these things, we think you'll find these recipes helpful in adding stress-free, gluten-free variety to your diet.

In our world, the best cookbooks are those that are born of a real-life cooking need, like this one. We hope that this book helps meet *your* need for delicious, wholesome, gluten-free meals that everyone in your family will enjoy.

—*Kimberly Mayone and Kitty Broihier, MS, RD*

Introduction

This is a cookbook for people who want to use their slow cookers to make gluten-free food. Even if you've never used a slow cooker or made gluten-free food before, you can easily use this cookbook and learn a few things about both topics in the process.

We are cookbook authors (and moms) who saw a need to combine gluten-free recipes with the slow cooking method in order to help people simplify their cooking lives and still produce great-tasting food for themselves and their families. Suggestions about where to find additional information on celiac disease and gluten intolerance, as well as gluten-free cooking in general, are included in Resources for Gluten-Free Living (see page 203).

Slow, Gluten-Free Cooking

There are several reasons why slow cooking is especially suitable for a gluten-free lifestyle. First, eating gluten-free isn't easy. It takes constant attention to ingredients and cooking techniques (to avoid cross-contamination, for example), requires diligent label reading, and may demand extra shopping trips because not all stores carry a wide range of appropriate ingredients. All of this takes time—something that is in short supply for most of us! Using a slow cooker to prepare gluten-free food makes the whole process safe, wholesome, and easy.

Secondly, gluten-free recipes incorporate a wider variety of grains than most people regularly eat. Slow cookers are great for cooking grains, which typically take a long time to cook. With a slow cooker doing all the work, there is no need to hang out in the kitchen waiting for millet or wild rice to finally finish cooking. You're free to do other things, even leave the house if you like. Slow cookers safely cook grains to perfection while you go about living your life. Of course, slow cookers also are convenient for cooking other gluten-free staples, such as meats, vegetables, and beans.

Another reason why slow cooking makes sense for those who avoid gluten is that it gives you complete control over the ingredients. Most of the recipes in this book utilize whole foods and very few processed foods. This is important because processed foods generally include ingredients that don't fit the gluten-free lifestyle. Slow cooking with wholesome, simple ingredients makes gluten avoiders feel more confident about what they're eating. And that leads to greater enjoyment at the table.

Finally, one of the main reasons we adore our slow cookers is that, with little effort, we can serve our families a real meal. There's something so comforting about coming home to the tempting aroma of a hot, home-cooked meal. For cooks who have children, putting together a slow cooker recipe is a nice way to do something fun and productive together. Slow cooker recipes are generally quite simple, providing a good introduction to cooking for little ones. With supervision, your child can learn to measure ingredients, use a knife safely, and even garnish and serve food with flourish and pride. Whether you use your slow cooker primarily for "soup night" or your favorite beef roast—or simply

to branch out from the usual gluten-free fare—cooking at home with a slow cooker brings a pleasurable ease to the dinner hour that is priceless.

About Our Recipes

Most of our recipes rely on whole foods and use mainstream ingredients. The recipes we've included range from straight-forward family-friendly fare to ethnic specialties to party food. In other words, we believe we've provided something for everyone in this book.

Cooking different foods for people in the same family to eat at the same meal takes too much time and effort, not to mention what it can do to the household food budget! This book contains recipes that everyone can enjoy—whether they are following a gluten-free diet or not.

COOKING TIMES For most of our recipes, cooking times are standardized to 8 to 10 hours on LOW or 4 to 5 hours on HIGH because these time frames seem to suit most people's lifestyles. There are some recipes that will not fit this formula, but are nonetheless suited to the slow cooking technique, including roasted nuts, egg dishes, and seafood dishes. In every case, we have done our utmost to make using a slow cooker as carefree as it's supposed to be, without requiring constant tending.

INGREDIENT AVAILABILITY We have made a serious effort to keep our recipes simple and the ingredients easily obtainable from most supermarkets. Slow cooker recipes should not be fussy. Happily, many of our essential slow cooking ingredients are already gluten-free. Other key ingredients, such as chicken broth, require gluten-free versions. Becoming familiar with the gluten-free section at your grocery store is required, but chances are you shop there already if you're living a gluten-free lifestyle or have cooked gluten-free recipes before. As we developed this book, we were thrilled to notice more and more gluten-free products on supermarket shelves. Indeed, the gluten-free foods trend is still on the upswing, and food manufacturers of all sizes are making a big effort to bring a wider range of gluten-free goods to market. A few of the ingredients we call for might necessitate a trip to the natural foods store (or some online shopping). But we don't often have time for multiple trips to multiple markets, so we are pretty sure you don't, either. Plus, the whole point of slow cooking is ease. Spending time chasing down exotic ingredients defeats that purpose.

SPECIFIED BRANDS If we think an ingredient or product in any of our recipes might contain gluten, we suggest a brand that is gluten-free. These brands are specified in the ingredient list in parentheses to make them easy to find. When purchasing foods that are processed in any way, it's essential to always double-check the labels for any gluten-containing ingredients.

RECIPE TIPS AND NOTES Finally, throughout the book, you'll notice various tips, notes, and tidbits of culinary information. We hope these added morsels will be helpful, educational, or, at the very least, interesting!

Dairy-Free Recipes

Although we don't claim that this book is tailored for those who have multiple food allergies, we realize that many people who follow a gluten-free diet also avoid dairy. Many of the recipes in this book are egg-, seafood-, and dairy-free. To make it easier to find dairy-free recipes and variations in the book, we have given them special symbols. Dark green leaves indicate dairy-free recipes, and pale green leaves mark recipes that can easily be made dairy-free with minor adjustments.

Note: *In the medical field and health world, eggs are treated as a separate allergen from dairy products such as milk and cheese, which explains why we have not grouped eggs with dairy products in this book. Most grocery stores, however, stock eggs with dairy products and refer to eggs as dairy products.*

Living Gluten-Free

Gluten, a protein found in wheat, rye, and barley, is ubiquitous in our food supply. In fact, some of the most common gluten-containing foods—breads, cereals, and noodles—are staples of our diet. What you might not know is that gluten is also found in many condiments, processed foods, and common kitchen supplies such as broths and spice mixtures.

Going gluten-free is not easy. It requires some study, plenty of patience, and lots of label reading. There's a steep learning curve associated with following a strict gluten-free diet, so a good dose of determination is also required. Nevertheless, a gluten-free "lifestyle" is achievable, and the diet itself is becoming easier to follow, thanks to the growing availability of commercial gluten-free foods.

Deciding to follow a gluten-free diet is not a choice to be taken lightly. In fact, for many people, it's not a *choice* at all. For those who have been diagnosed with celiac disease, an autoimmune disorder (or its cousin, gluten intolerance), being thrust into a gluten-free diet is frequently a shocking reality. For them, avoiding gluten is vitally important—a medical necessity, in fact—not just a fad or health food trend. Giving yourself a diagnosis of a gluten problem of any sort is not recommended. A haphazard gluten-free lifestyle can lead to nutritional imbalances and nutrient deficiencies over time. These conditions are real and serious. A proper medical evaluation and diagnosis are essential for developing a comprehensive treatment plan.

Some people choose to follow a gluten-free diet for nonmedical reasons, however. Perhaps the diet helps them focus on whole grains and reduce their consumption of

1

processed carbohydrates. Some people claim they have more energy when they don't eat gluten-containing foods (this could be because they're avoiding highly processed carbs and instead eating complex carbs that provide sustained energy, as opposed to a quick spike). Others say they just feel better overall when they abstain from gluten. Some people think a gluten-free diet will help them lose weight. Unfortunately, that's not always true. In fact, many people gain some weight on a gluten-free diet (especially if they actually have a gluten-related disorder and were not digesting food properly before starting a gluten-free diet). Whatever the reason for your interest in gluten-free living, we highly recommend consulting a registered dietitian (RD) in order to learn how to eat a nutritious, well-rounded diet while avoiding gluten-containing foods.

If you're going to go gluten-free, do it right. Educate yourself and seek help from experts. While this book is a cookbook and not a medical manual, we think it's important to provide some basic information about celiac disease and gluten intolerance, as well as a very basic "how-to" for gluten-free eating.

Gluten-Free? Why Me?

Celiac disease is not a new disease by any means, but it is now recognized as much more prevalent than anyone knew. Thanks to improved diagnostic tests, it's now estimated that celiac disease affects about 1 out of 100 people in the United States and European countries (1 out of 266 people worldwide). Aside from better diagnostic testing procedures, most experts believe that there are other reasons for the uptick in prevalence of celiac disease and gluten-related conditions. More study is under way to determine what these causative factors might be.

Celiac disease is an autoimmune disorder. "Autoimmune" means that the body is triggered to abnormally "attack" itself. Celiac disease has a strong genetic component. Basically, when genetically susceptible individuals eat gluten proteins, their immune systems react strongly and cause inflammation in the small intestine. Over time, this inflammation damages the absorptive lining of the intestine, which can lead to malabsorption of a number of nutrients and further health problems. Many people with celiac disease suffer from a wide variety of symptoms (not all of which are gastrointestinal), while other people have "silent" celiac disease, in which symptoms are nonexistent or so subtle as to go undetected. It used to be thought that celiac disease began in early childhood, but now experts recognize that it can develop at any time.

The term "gluten intolerance" is recognized by experts in the field of gluten diseases, but its definition is not agreed upon. It's generally accepted that those people who develop celiac-like symptoms when exposed to gluten but do not have any immune reaction are gluten intolerant.

Consuming gluten makes these people feel bad, but their intestines are not damaged by it and the diagnostic tests for celiac disease show normal functioning. Nevertheless, these gluten intolerant people do suffer real symptoms and therefore find a gluten-free diet helpful. Gluten "sensitivity" is not a diagnostic term; rather, it refers to the group of gluten-related disorders.

For many people, finally getting a diagnosis for a disease that's been making them feel terrible, sometimes for years, is a relief; what soon follows, however, can be frightening. The treatment for celiac disease, as well as for gluten intolerance, is avoidance of gluten—for life. Being told that you must now follow a strict diet may seem like a punishment. What's more, the initial impression of the diet is that it's confusing, limiting, daunting, and even depressing. However, it needn't be any of these things.

As a matter of fact, there are some great things about the gluten-free lifestyle that you may not have considered. One of the major benefits is that you'll learn to incorporate a wide range of alternate grains into your diet. Whole grains are excellent sources of much-needed fiber, as well as nutrients including protein, B vitamins, iron, and other important minerals. A typical U.S. diet falls short on whole grains, but contains plenty of highly processed grains and grain-based foods. Experts recommend that you aim to get half of your day's intake of grains and grain-based foods as whole grains. By its very nature, gluten-free eating emphasizes more healthful carbohydrates over refined carbohydrates. Your body prefers the long-lasting energy that complex carbohydrates provide. What's more, foods that feature "healthy carbs" are typically more healthful all around, containing more nutrients than foods made predominantly from refined carbs, such as cakes, cookies, pastries, and other treats. A gluten-free eating plan can also encourage you to eat more produce. Fruits and vegetables are frequently found to be lacking in the typical American diet. However, since they are inherently gluten-free, including more of them in cooking is an easy way to fill out a meal while also boosting consumption of vitamins, minerals, and fiber. Fruits and vegetables also contain beneficial phytonutrients, such as the well-known carotenoids (including beta-carotene) in carrots, pumpkin, and sweet potatoes; lutein in leafy greens; lycopene in tomato products (among others); and a variety of polyphenols and flavonoids found in numerous fruits and vegetables.

In order to follow a gluten-free diet well, you must become knowledgeable. To do that requires expert help. In most cases, a physician will provide a diagnosis, but not the practical instructions necessary to follow a gluten-free diet. Here's where the registered dietitian comes in. Consulting with an RD who is also an expert in celiac disease and gluten-free living is the best way to cope with a diagnosis of celiac disease. The RD will provide the information, tools, suggestions, and usually even the recipes you need to make a gluten-free diet understandable and achievable. Your physician can refer you to an appropriate dietitian, or you can locate one through the American Dietetic Association website, www.eatright.org.

In addition, numerous excellent resources about gluten-free diets are available at libraries, bookstores, and online (see Resources for Gluten-Free Living on page 203). Support groups can also be very helpful when learning to go gluten-free. In order to understand some of the ingredient choices in this cookbook, a basic grasp of what constitutes a gluten-free eating plan is helpful.

What Exactly Is a Gluten-Free Diet?

The primary concern in a gluten-free diet is grains—specifically, avoiding grains and grain-based foods that contain gluten. Below you'll find lists of grains and grain-based ingredients that are considered safe and unsafe for a gluten-free eating plan:

UNSAFE GRAINS
AND GRAIN PRODUCTS

WHEAT

- bulgur
  (*also called cracked wheat*)
- durum
- farina
- farro
- kamut
- semolina
- spelt
- triticale (*a cross between wheat and rye*)
- wheat berries, wheat bran, wheat flour, wheat germ, wheat starch

OTHER GRAIN PRODUCTS

- rye bread
- rye flour
- barley, pearl barley
- regular beer and ale (*some gluten-free beers are now available*)
- brewer's yeast
- malt vinegar
- malted milk, malt extract, malt syrup
- oats (*unless specifically tested and labeled as gluten-free*), oatmeal, oat bran, oat flour

SAFE GRAINS
AND GRAIN PRODUCTS

- amaranth
- buckwheat
- corn, cornmeal
- millet
- quinoa
- rice (*brown, white*)
- teff (*a grass that produces grain—a staple in Ethiopia, available at health food stores*)
- wild rice
- flours and starches made from gluten-free sources: arrowroot, corn, potato, soy, tapioca

OTHER SAFE FOODS THAT SUPPORT A GLUTEN-FREE DIET

DAIRY PRODUCTS: milk, cream, buttermilk, plain yogurt, cottage cheese, plain cheeses, ice cream (unless it contains gluten-containing ingredients)

MEAT, POULTRY, FISH AND EGGS: fresh or frozen meat, poultry, and fish. (Brined, seasoned, or broth-injected meat products frequently contain gluten and are therefore not safe.)

BEANS: dried beans and canned beans processed without gluten-containing ingredients (check product label)

SEEDS: sesame, sunflower, and pumpkin

NUTS: Plain nuts that are raw and unseasoned or roasted and unseasoned are safe. If nuts are present in a mixture or are seasoned in any way, check the label. Avoid purchasing nuts from open bins where cross-contamination with gluten-containing products may occur.

TOFU: considered "safe," but sometimes contains gluten. As always, check labels and do not purchase tofu that is unlabeled.

FRUIT: fresh, frozen, canned, and some dried varieties (check product labels on dried fruits)

VEGETABLES: fresh, frozen, or canned (unless processed with gluten-containing ingredients)

Using grains safely

Some gluten-free grains may be cross-contaminated with other grains, such as wheat and barley, for example, because of how they're grown, harvested, processed, or packaged. To be safe, here are a few rules to follow:

• Purchase only gluten-free grains and flours that are specifically labeled "gluten-free."

• Do not assume that a product labeled "organic" is gluten-free. An organic product can still be contaminated.

• When a manufacturer has a gluten-free line of products, but doesn't include a particular product in that line, even though it might seem appropriate—there's a reason. Don't purchase that product.

• Be aware that vague labeling such as "made with gluten-free ingredients" or "no gluten ingredients used" is not the same as a trustworthy gluten-free label. It's likely that the manufacturer does not test its products for gluten contamination.

FATS: butter, margarine, nut oils, vegetable oils

SWEETS: honey, jam, jelly, maple syrup, molasses, sugar

Within these general food groups, there are many variations and exceptions. For detailed information on specific foods that are allowed and not allowed on a gluten-free diet, consult a registered dietitian or keep an up-to-date reference book handy (see Resources for Gluten-Free Living, page 203).

An Important Caveat about Oats

Although oats are inherently gluten-free, they can be cross-contaminated with wheat and barley because of how they're grown, harvested, processed, or packaged. Although the amount of cross-contamination varies, most celiac organizations advise against consuming *any* oat products. Now, however, uncontaminated gluten-free oats are available in both retail and online outlets from certain companies in North America. Oats contribute fiber, needed nutrients, and variety to a gluten-free diet. Seek out sources of uncontaminated oats—their labels will carry a gluten-free claim. Companies should be forthcoming about the method of gluten testing they employ (the highly sensitive R5-ELISA test is the best available test right now) and the steps they take to keep the product safe and gluten-free. If they are confident about the safety of their products, they will happily share information with you. If they don't come across with that information, don't purchase their products. To be safe, always purchase only pure, uncontaminated oats. These oats will be labeled as gluten-free. Before you add oats to your gluten-free diet, consult your physician or dietitian for guidelines. If you have celiac disease, don't add oats to your diet unless the disease is well controlled.

Saying Goodbye to Gluten

One of the first steps you'll take on your journey to gluten-free living is locating and purchasing gluten-free foods and cooking ingredients. Many gluten-free foods are already stocked at your local supermarket, either in the regular aisles or in the "healthy," "natural," or, if you're lucky, "gluten-free" aisle. There are also numerous online sources of gluten-free foods and ingredients (see Chapter 4, "The Gluten-Free Pantry," page 27).

In order to save time at the supermarket, it's a good idea to research the foods you most commonly use via the Internet. Many food manufacturers now post specific food allergy information about their products on their product websites. This information may not always be conclusive (websites are not always up to date), but it will red-flag ingredients that contain gluten. If a website doesn't specify if a particular item contains gluten, check the label at the store or consider sending an email inquiry to the manufacturer. Regardless, double-checking labels at the store is a must-do for the gluten-intolerant consumer. Labels are always the most updated source of ingredient information.

When you first start shopping for acceptable foods, expect the process to take longer than it used to before you began your gluten-free lifestyle. It does take considerable time to check the labels on all processed food packages for sources of gluten, but you *will* get more efficient at it. One way to speed things up a bit is to take along a "cheat sheet." This can be a pocket-sized guide to gluten-free food brands, a household-specific shopping list of safe foods that you've compiled yourself, or even a celiac-specific software program or "app" for your smartphone.

Finally, get over any inhibitions you may have about calling food manufacturers directly on the telephone. This is why they have consumer hotlines and consumer affairs specialists, who probably get asked about gluten dozens of times a day! In many cases the company's phone number is right there on the label. If not, check the brand's website. The growing interest in gluten-free foods has prompted many manufacturers to provide that information on their product websites.

Label Reading for Eating Gluten-Free

We've said it before in this book and you'll no doubt hear it many more times: reading labels is key for eating gluten-free. There's no substitute for the consistent reading of labels, since manufacturers are required to indicate all food ingredients on the label's ingredient list. Read the labels each and every time you purchase the food item, since manufacturers often change their formulations (recipes) for a variety of reasons. They are not required to tell the consumer that they have changed any of the ingredients, so it's up to you to read the label every time.

To read the label, first check for any obvious wheat, rye, or barley ingredients. Next, look for a "contains" statement on the label—for example, "contains wheat." All packaged food products regulated by the

U.S. Food and Drug Administration (FDA) must clearly declare the presence of wheat—or protein derived from wheat—in the ingredient list. If a wheat-based ingredient doesn't already include the word "wheat" in it, then a "contains wheat" statement must appear on the label. (Incidentally, this rule also applies to seven other major food allergens: fish, shellfish, tree nuts, peanuts, milk, eggs, and soybeans.) Here are two examples of FDA-approved labeling:

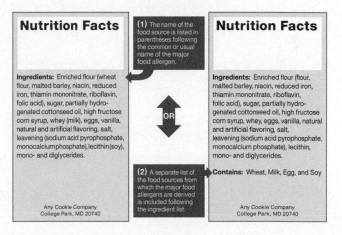

Here is a list of some ingredients that *contain* wheat and require a "contains wheat" statement on the label:

- durum flour
- enriched flour
- farina
- graham flour
- self-rising flour
- semolina

Some ingredients may be, but are not always, derived from wheat. In the United States, ingredient lists must put the word "wheat" in parentheses following those ingredients, or a separate "contains wheat" statement must follow the ingredient list on the package label. Examples of ingredients that may or may not be wheat-derived include (but are not limited to)

- caramel color
- dextrin
- flavorings
- modified food starch
- seasoning mixtures
- spice blends

Planning Gluten-Free Meals

Here are some ideas to make planning gluten-free meals easier:

- **Plan meals ahead of time.** Saturday and Sunday are great days for meal planning because supermarket circulars usually come out on Friday. If you have a flexible schedule, consider shopping on Monday or Tuesday mornings when stores are typically less crowded.

- **Focus on plain, simple foods at first.** Then, as you grow more comfortable with shopping for and preparing gluten-free meals, you can work in a few more convenience items, multiple-ingredient recipes, and specific gluten-free versions of staple foods.

- **Don't forget to put snacks on your shopping list.** It's always a good idea to keep safe snack foods handy in your car, purse, or gym bag and in the kids' backpacks, lunch boxes, or lockers at school. When you're hungry or just craving something to munch on, you need those safe snacks on hand. Aside from fresh fruit and veggies, cheese, and plain nuts, consider laying in a supply of gluten-free snack foods such as pretzels, plain tortilla chips, popcorn, and rice cakes. You'll be amazed at the variety of snack foods you can eat when you make a habit of reading the labels.

- **Incorporate a wide variety of fresh produce in your recipes.** Fruits and vegetables are naturally gluten-free, super healthy, and generally low in calories and fat. Best of all, fresh produce adds lots of flavor and texture to your meals. Let it shine in your cooking.

- **Start collecting your favorite gluten-free recipes** and put them in a binder, instead of taking the time to search through piles of magazines and recipe files to find what you want. A recipe binder will also be helpful to others who may want to cook *for* you!

For more ideas and brand-specific suggestions for gluten-free food items, check out Chapter 4, "The Gluten-Free Pantry," page 27, as well as "Resources for Gluten-Free Living," page 203. Many of these publications include extensive lists of food companies that produce gluten-free foods (and their addresses, phone numbers, and websites) as well as meal-planning ideas, sample menus, and recipes that make gluten-free cooking easier.

Keeping Your Gluten-Free Food Safe to Eat

After you've spent time researching, shopping, and lugging home all your carefully selected, gluten-free foods, you don't want them to spoil. Learning how to store and handle these foods properly is key, not only for you, but for everyone in your household. Here's why: when a gluten-containing food comes in contact with a gluten-free food, cross-contamination occurs. In other words, gluten can be transferred from one food to any other food inadvertently—and quite easily. Cross-contamination can occur anywhere food is prepared, stored, served, or eaten.

Food manufacturers are attentive to the possibility of cross-contamination and are required to take steps in order to prevent it. At the very least, a thorough washing of equipment between the processing of gluten-containing foods and the processing of gluten-free foods is necessary. Some manufacturers use separate production lines for gluten-free products, while others use dedicated facilities that process gluten-free items exclusively.

People who are concerned about gluten cross-contamination generally focus on foods prepared or eaten outside of the home, such as at a restaurant, school, or workplace. This is a very serious concern, since the consumer has virtually no control over the situation. Cooking utensils such as scoops, spatulas, spoons, and knives, as well as cooking equipment such as grills, pans, and deep-fat fryers can transfer gluten from one food to the next food prepared with the same utensils or cooked with the same equipment. Most diners don't think twice about whether the spatula that flipped someone else's grilled cheese sandwich was then used to flip their burger patty. But for people who are gluten-sensitive, this type of worry surfaces every time they eat away from home. As a result, many people who avoid gluten don't eat out unless absolutely necessary.

The possibility of cross-contamination isn't limited by any means to foods eaten away from home. Your own kitchen presents many opportunities for contaminating your food with gluten. Once you become aware of situations and cooking behaviors that may contribute to cross-contamination, you'll begin to find practical solutions for preventing it. Eventually, these safety measures will become second nature to you and your family. Here are a few considerations:

• Make a habit of thoroughly washing counters and other cooking surfaces before cooking gluten-free foods.

• Differentiate gluten-free food from other foods in the house, either by storing it in a separate cupboard or shelf in the refrigerator or by marking it somehow (or both).

- Separate food that may easily become cross-contaminated (such as butter or margarine, jelly and peanut butter) from other foods in the house.

- Pots and pans that are used for regular food need to be thoroughly washed and scrubbed before coming in contact with gluten-free ingredients. The same goes for cooking utensils and knives.

- Get a separate set of baking utensils and equipment to avoid cross-contamination. Using disposable bakeware for gluten-free items can be helpful.

- Keep a separate cutting board for gluten-free foods.

- Buy a second toaster to use only for gluten-free foods.

- Cook gluten-free foods before regular foods if you need to use the same pan.

Get Plugged In to the Gluten-Free Community

There's no need to feel isolated when you've been diagnosed with a gluten-related disorder. You're certainly not alone, and there is plenty of help available when it comes to navigating the specifics of gluten-free diets, shopping strategies, meal planning, and cooking techniques. Here are a few suggestions for connecting with people and resources that can help you cope with all aspects of your gluten-free lifestyle:

- Consult a registered dietitian for help with your diet and for recommendations about local stores to shop in, new foods to try (coupons are frequently available through dietitians), and gluten-free cooking classes in your area.

- Search on the Internet for local gluten-sensitivity support groups in your area. These organizations have regular meetings, offer social activities, and are good places to make some new friends who are also dealing with gluten-related issues.

- Subscribe to one or more of the magazines tailored to consumers with food allergies, such as *Living Without, Easy Eats, and Gluten-Free Living.* Not only do they contain informative articles, but they're usually packed with recipes, helpful cooking tips, and advertisements for new gluten-free foods you can find at the market. These magazines may also be available at your local library, and past issues and features may be posted on the magazines' websites.

- Check out some of the many gluten-free blogs. Find one (or a few) that you like—once you subscribe you'll start to receive email alerts to the newest posts and recipes.

- See Resources for Gluten-Free Living, page 203, for a list of organizations, books, magazines, blogs, websites, and other information resources and products that support gluten-free living and cooking.

2
Slow Cooking 101

Chances are, if you're reading this book you already own a slow cooker and want to make better use of it for gluten-free cooking. On the other hand, maybe you just received a slow cooker as a gift—lucky you!—or recently came across your own machine (maybe the one you received as a wedding gift) in the back of a cupboard, and you haven't the foggiest idea how to use it. Whatever the scenario, this chapter covers the basics of slow cooking, from its first appearance on the culinary scene to the various types of cookers on the market to the "Ten Commandments" of slow cooking. If you're new to the world of slow-cooked food, this is required reading.

A Quick Intro to Slow Cooking

The first commercial slow cooker arrived on the culinary scene in 1971, when Rival introduced its Crock-Pot®, a modification of its bean-cooking pot. Within four years of its introduction, the Crock-Pot® had achieved $93 million in sales—testament to its novelty certainly, but also to its ease of use. Here was an appliance that practically ensured that anyone who used it would produce not just an edible meal, but a delicious one, without having to actually cook and tend to the food.

Other appliance makers soon were selling their own versions of the Crock-Pot® under various brand names, and the appliances became known generically as slow cookers. (For many people, the name "Crock-Pot®" is interchangeable with the term "slow cooker," but to avoid a tangle with the legal department at Rival, we prefer to use the nontrademarked "slow cooker.") Slow cooker sales slumped in the 1980s, but in the last several years the category has rebounded and seen abundant diversification and a trend toward a more upscale product. So while slow cooker styles, colors, sizes, features, and brands have changed over forty years, we continue to rely on slow cookers for easy, satisfying meals. This is a piece of cooking equipment that shows no signs of losing its place on kitchen countertops any time soon.

If the last time you even looked at a slow cooker was when your mother or grandmother hauled her avocado-colored (or burnt orange) crock out of the closet to make her famous onion-soup pot roast, you're in for a surprise. Slow cookers have come a long way since then! In fact, there is now a wide variety of brands and sizes of cookers available at all price points. Even high-end kitchen equipment manufacturers have embraced the slow cooking concept, with the price tag for these machines reflecting their elite slow cooker "status."

Slow cookers are in stock at a wide variety of stores, including "big box" retailers, department stores, and cookware stores. You can also pick up a good deal on last year's slow cooker models at a discount store. And, of course, online shopping is convenient and can yield some great deals, especially if you use a price comparison website or overstock/discount retailer. Check out manufacturers' websites for specific information and available models so you'll know what you want when it comes time to purchase your machine. (For a list of manufacturers' websites, see Resources for Gluten-Free Living, page 203).

In general, slow cookers are not complicated appliances, and they all work in about the same way. The stoneware crock sits in a metal housing that's fitted with an electric heating element. When turned on, the crock heats, a vacuum is created in the covered crock, and the food cooks at a low temperature (just around boiling, or 212°F) over a period of hours. Pretty simple stuff, really. In our opinion, that's the beauty of it. A simple machine with two heat settings—low and high—can produce great-tasting slow-cooked food just as well as a fancy slow cooker.

Characteristics to Consider

Most slow cookers that we've come across are of the continuous heating variety, as opposed to those that use a heat cycling mechanism to maintain temperature. Both types work just fine, so it doesn't really matter which one you choose. There are a number of other characteristics that we find much more important when determining which slow cooker to purchase or how to make the best use of the slow cooker you already own.

IS THE CROCK REMOVABLE OR FIXED?

Aside from the mini-crocks used for dips, most new slow cooker models have removable crock inserts, and it's not hard to figure out why: they are infinitely more practical than the older fixed-crock types. A removable crock is easier to clean (either by hand or in the dishwasher), it can be used on its own as a serving dish, and some crocks can be used on the stove-top (handy for browning meat prior to slow cooking) or in the oven (check the manual first to be sure yours is suitable for this type of cooking). Fixed-crock machines are hard to clean (you cannot put the whole thing in a pan of water or the dishwasher because of the heating element and cord), and they are generally smaller in size than those with removable crocks.

If you have a fixed-crock cooker, it's probably quite old. Nevertheless, if it still works and cleaning it doesn't bother you, by all means keep using it! If you're looking to purchase a new one, however, it is likely to have a removable crock (all newer models do) and an array of other important features, depending on the brand and model.

WHAT SIZE IS MOST PRACTICAL FOR YOU?

Slow cookers range in size and capacity from about two cups to a whopping seven quarts. The small machines are appropriate for dips and sauces (perfect for entertaining), while the larger slow cookers can easily roast a chicken—even two if they're small! Medium-sized models (2½- to 4-quart capacity) are perfect for singles and couples, while the larger capacity models (5- to 7-quart) are appropriate for families and cooking for a crowd. Our favorite slow cooker size is a 5-quart, which holds just about everything we want to cook for our families of three to five people, is easy to handle and store, and doesn't take up much space on the counter.

Give some thought to the types of recipes you'd like to cook. Are you interested in primarily making soups and stews? A large model might work for you even if you have a small family, since leftovers can usually be frozen for another night (or refrigerated for lunches later in the week). If you plan on using your machine mostly for entertaining, go with a larger model. You may even come across a two-for-one deal pairing a large crock with a smaller one (frequently these can be found in stores around the holidays). This arrangement could cover your party needs from dips to double batches of your favorite chili.

WHICH SHAPE SUITS YOUR COOKING NEEDS?

As for shape, oval, round, and rounded rectangular crocks all have their merits. Round crocks are fine for soups, mixed dishes, and small cuts of meat and poultry. The oval shape is our favorite and the most popular shape these days. It does everything a round crock can do, but also accommodates large roasts and whole poultry more easily. The newer rounded rectangle fits nicely in a cupboard for storage or tucked into the corner of your kitchen countertop for ready access. It also is suitable for cooking multiple small birds.

The color of the slow cooker housing is also a consideration. If you are going to stash your cooker in a cupboard or elsewhere, where it will be out of sight when not in use, color may be of no concern to you. On the other hand, if it will be a permanent fixture on your counter, you'll want an attractive machine that complements your kitchen decor. Machines with a stainless-steel finish are popular now because they look modern and professional. Black is a classic, go-with-anything choice. Whichever color and shape you choose, be sure you like it. Most slow cookers last for many years, so you'll be cooking in it (and looking at it) for a good, long time.

WHAT FEATURES ARE IMPORTANT TO YOU?

While most slow cookers are fairly simple in design and are appropriate for most people's needs, some upscale models offer additional features that can either take your slow cooking experience to the next level or create needless complications. For example, delay settings, digital controls, programmable cooking cycles, touch pads instead of knobs, travel and portability features, and even preprogrammed recipes are all currently available. A relative newcomer to the slow cooker scene is a combination slow cooker and rice cooker. Most of these have multiple crocks and steamer baskets or bowls that are interchanged in the cooker, depending on what you're cooking.

All these features add to the machine's cost, of course, and since one of the benefits of slow cooking is that it's usually a very cost-effective method of cooking, an expensive machine might not make sense. Fancy features can be fun, but be sure you'll actually use them before plunking down your money—fancy machines can cost up to $200, while a simple slow cooker can be had for about $20. And keep in mind that a basic machine with two or three heat settings and a removable crock insert is all you really need to produce wonderful slow-cooked meals for you and your family.

The Ten Commandments of Slow Cooking

These are the most important general rules for slow cooking. (Safety information is discussed on page 16.)

1. Plan ahead for slow cooking. Since the general idea of slow cooking is to let the food cook by itself while you go about your daily business, it's essential to have all ingredients on hand and ready to put into the crock in the morning (unless it's a quick-cooking recipe that can be started later in the day and still be ready in time for dinner). An unplanned trip to the supermarket for ingredients takes away from the time-savings that slow cooking provides. Check the ingredient list at least the day before, so you can thaw meat or poultry safely in the refrigerator, and consider prepping ingredients the night before. In the morning all you will need to do is put everything into the crock, plug it in, turn it on, and scoot out the door!

2. Coat the inside of the crock with gluten-free cooking spray, oil, or butter if there's even a chance that cleanup will be a chore. A good part of the allure of slow cooking is that it's easy—spending hours soaking and scrubbing afterward doesn't fit into our definition of "easy." Serving foods, such as dips or soups, directly from the slow cooker cuts down on dirty dishes as well.

3. If using vegetables with varying densities, layer the densest ones on the bottom and work up to the least dense. In many recipes this means that the carrots or potatoes go on the bottom, and veggies like celery, onions, leeks, and tomatoes will be layered on top. This method will ensure that all the veggies are thoroughly cooked.

4. Cut ingredients for mixed dishes into similar-sized pieces so everything cooks relatively evenly. Big pieces of carrot will take longer to cook than finely chopped carrots. The same rule applies to all vegetables (onions, celery, and potatoes, for example).

5. Always trim fat from meat and poultry before slow cooking. Not only will this cut down on your fat intake, but it also makes the final dish more appealing. For example, when slow cooking chicken thighs, remove and discard the skin or simply buy boneless, skinless thighs in the first place.

6. Brown ground meat before adding it to the slow cooker (except for meatloaf recipes). If you don't, the finished product will be greasy and less than appetizing.

7. Fill the slow cooker crock one-half to two-thirds full for the best results. These machines are designed to perform best when they're not over- or underfilled. An underfilled crock is more likely to overcook the food, while a crock that's too full is obviously more likely to spill over and present a danger (not to mention a mess). If you find that you're consistently cooking too little or too much in your crock, consider trading up or down in size so your slow cooker is more appropriate for your needs.

8. Do not lift the lid of the slow cooker unless instructed to do so in the recipe. Continually peeking at the food won't make it cook faster. In fact, a lot of heat is lost each time the lid is removed, which can make the food take longer to cook.

9. Choose low and slow whenever you can. They don't call it a slow cooker for nothing! Frequently the best flavors and textures in slow-cooked foods are achieved after a long cooking time on the low setting. This does not mean that things can never be speeded up a bit if necessary. In general, cooking on the high setting takes about half the time that cooking on low does (although this isn't a foolproof rule since ingredients are a factor as well). Always check for doneness when going the speedy route.

10. Don't sweat the sauce. Because moisture in a slow cooker does not evaporate the way it does with stove-top cooking, slow-cooked recipes sometimes seem to have an excess of liquid. Do not fret! Ladle some of the liquid over the food and call it "sauce," if appropriate, or you can mix a little cornstarch with a small amount of cold water or broth and whisk it in, cover the crock, and cook on high heat for a few minutes until it thickens into "gravy." Another option is to save the cooking liquid—it's frequently very flavorful—and use it as a base for soup another day. Or simply discard it.

Be Safe, Not Sorry

Like any electrical kitchen appliance, a slow cooker needs to be treated with care and used as intended if it's to perform in a satisfactory and safe manner. So here's the lowdown on how to handle your cooker and safely cook the food you place inside it. A few minutes spent reviewing these tips will pay you back many times over in the form of tasty, wholesome meals.

Read the manual that came with your slow cooker—don't throw it away! You know how it is. In all the excitement of using your new kitchen gadget, you barely even notice the instruction manual that came with it. That's a mistake for several reasons. First, your new machine may not work properly and you may need some troubleshooting suggestions. You may need to return your slow cooker to the store where you purchased it, and the manual should go with it. If you staple the receipt for your slow cooker to the manual and jot down the date and location of purchase on the inside front cover, you'll be ready if your machine needs to be returned or repaired. The manual will have information *specific* to your machine—for instance, safety steps you need to take the first time you use it, or how to set any programmable features. If your machine is old and you no longer have the manual (or you inadvertently tossed it in your zeal to start cooking in your brand-new slow cooker), check the manufacturer's website for a printable copy of the instruction booklet.

Handle the slow cooker crock carefully. Rough treatment, such as knocking the crock against the counter or kitchen faucet, may crack or chip it. Always inspect the crock and lid for cracks and chipped surfaces before you use it, since any defect can become worse during cooking, resulting in a mess—and a lost meal. To minimize damage, allow the crock to cool completely before washing it, whether you're hand-washing it or putting it in the dishwasher. Most removable crocks are dishwasher safe, but some manufacturers recommend hand-washing. Minimize the need for scrubbing by using gluten-free, nonstick cooking spray, butter, or oil to grease the inside of the crock before cooking. If you still need to really scrub the surface of the crock, let it soak in warm water first; then use a plastic scouring pad. If you have a defective crock or lid, consult the manufacturer's website or the manual for instructions on obtaining a replacement.

Avoid exposing the slow cooker crock to sudden changes in temperature. In other words, don't add frozen or very cold ingredients to a hot crock or you'll risk it cracking. Similarly, avoid adding boiling hot food to a very cold crock. Either cool down the liquid first, or warm up the crock by running warm water over and into it. In addition, do not put a crock full of hot food directly into the refrigerator. Instead, transfer leftover slow-cooked food to another dish (or divide it between multiple containers) for refrigeration. Always remove leftover food from the crock as soon as you're finished eating or within one hour at most in order to minimize the length of time the food stays in the "danger zone"—the range of temperature (40–140°F) in which any dangerous bacteria present in the leftover food can quickly multiply and cause illness when the leftovers are later consumed. Cooked food should be transferred to a separate container for refrigeration, not stored in the slow cooker crock in the refrigerator. This speeds cooling and is a common food safety practice. In addition, slow cooker crocks tend to retain some heat, which may cause the food to remain in an unsafe temperature range for too long. And finally, putting a warm crock into a cold refrigerator increases the chance that the crock will crack. Leftovers should not be reheated in a slow cooker—use the microwave or heat on the stove-top or in the oven. If you'd like to serve reheated leftovers in the slow cooker, bring them up to a temperature of 165°F and then transfer them to the slow cooker.

Slow cookers get very hot; take precautions! Although slow cookers are safe appliances and you needn't worry about leaving them at home alone to cook, they do get very hot during cooking. Be sure that the housing isn't touching anything else on the counter before you leave the room or house. While in use, be sure to place the slow cooker out of the reach of little hands. If the cord or plug is damaged in any way or looks loose or frayed, do not use the machine. Do not touch the slow cooker base during cooking, and place the cooker safely away from the edge of the counter so that it can't be knocked off the counter by accident while it's full of hot food. Oven mitts are required for removing a hot crock from the base and also for grasping the handle of the lid, since it can get quite hot as well.

Resist the temptation to assemble recipes in the slow cooker crock and then refrigerate it overnight. This is not a safe practice. A refrigerated crock is more likely to crack when heated. Thaw frozen ingredients in the refrigerator a day ahead or in the microwave on the "defrost" setting, according to the microwave's instruction manual, and then refrigerate ingredients until it is time to assemble them in the crock. Prepping ingredients the night before and then refrigerating them is fine (in fact, we strongly encourage this step), but leave the empty crock in the base at room temperature, ready for cooking the next morning.

Avoid putting frozen meat, fish, or poultry directly into the slow cooker. It's not safe for the crock, it can take a long time for the food to reach a safe temperature, and it adds hours to the cooking time. You can safely thaw frozen food in the refrigerator one day ahead of cooking it—and it takes even less time to thaw food in the microwave—so there's really no reason to add frozen food to the crock at all.

Play it safe. Get in the habit of using an "instant read" thermometer. They're super-easy to use and widely available. Here are the temperature recommendations that the U.S. Department of Agriculture suggests for various kinds of meat and poultry:

Beef, veal, lamb
  Roasts and steaks = 145°–160°F
  Ground = 160°F

Pork
  Roasts and chops = 160°F

Poultry
  Whole bird = 165°F
    (*insert thermometer into thigh*)
  Breasts, legs, thighs = 165°F
  Ground = 165°F

Tips for Gluten-Free Slow Cooking

3

Here is the good news: once you have become a label reader and your pantry is stocked with safe, gluten-free ingredients, slow cooking is easy. There are, however, several techniques, tricks, and "insider secrets" that will make slow cooking even easier and more successful. Of course, we rely on certain gluten-free ingredients again and again, and you will find your favorites, too. For a quick list of staples we like, check Chapter 4, "The Gluten-Free Pantry" (page 27).

Gluten-Free Slow Cooking Staples

BROTH Broth is an important ingredient in slow cooking because it provides depth and flavor to recipes. There are some gluten-free broths widely available, though you could also make your own at home. Bouillon is also used in many slow cooker recipes to increase flavor, especially in vegetable-heavy recipes. Certain vegetables like onions and celery will impart a large amount of liquid as they cook, and the bouillon will enhance this liquid. It is like making stock at the same time you cook dinner.

SALT Salt is one of the most important ingredients in any type of cooking. Kosher salt is our "go-to" salt but we also like sea salts and mineral salts. Kosher salt is budget-friendly and universally available. Often when a recipe is not quite right, all it needs is another pinch of salt. Keeping in mind good health and the overall need to moderate sodium intake, we aim to use the minimum amount of salt necessary to achieve great flavor in our recipes. Also, we prefer to salt at the beginning of cooking so that all the ingredients benefit from seasoning. If you would like to cut the salt in our recipes even further, feel free to do so, but realize that the dish may need other seasonings to make up for the decreased sodium. Some experimentation is necessary before you'll become adept at guesstimating how much salt and other seasonings to use in low-sodium dishes, so forgive yourself if your first attempts aren't stellar. Tasting a dish before you serve it will let you know if it needs additional seasoning. It's always easier to add more seasoning than it is to mask the taste of an oversalted or overseasoned dish.

ACIDS Vinegars, citrus juices, and hot sauces offer an acidic component to dishes. Like salt, acid is a flavor enhancer. We love the power of these three ingredients (alone or combined) to brighten flavors. Do not be afraid of hot sauces! Some are not all that spicy yet can really perk up a slow-cooked dish. One of our favorite finds while working on this book was Green Jalapeño Pepper Sauce made by Tabasco®—it's zingy but not too spicy!

FRESH HERBS Adding fresh, brightly flavored herbs to a dish can easily boost it from good to great (and makes it look fabulous, too). After a long, slow cook, the aromatic qualities of fresh herbs pull the dish together and bring it up to chef standards. For example, the cilantro and scallions used in Shrimp and Scallop Thai Curry (see page 107) are as important as the coconut milk in achieving the right Thai flavor—just like you'd expect at your favorite Thai restaurant. In many recipes, we list herbs as optional; in others they are part of the ingredient list.

THICKENERS It's the nature of slow cooking that liquid is generated during the cooking process. In some recipes we encourage you to use this liquid as a sauce to moisten meat. Using wheat flour to thicken sauces and gravies is out of the question, of course, but there are a few other options that make good use of cooking juices as gravy or sauce. For example, quick-cooking tapioca, cornstarch, and cornmeal (when appropriate) all work well to thicken cooking liquids. In some soup recipes, rice, beans, and starchy vegetables (such as sweet potatoes, peas, potatoes, winter squash) can be pureed to make the finished product thick and smooth. Grain, seed, and bean flours can also be used as thickeners, but in this book we've made a point to stick with ingredients we know are universally available.

Adapting Gluten-Free Favorites to the Slow Cooker

If there's a great stove-top recipe you'd like to prepare in your slow cooker, you'll undoubtedly find it either in this book or online, but if you want to adapt one of *your own* favorite recipes to slow cooking, you'll need to do some experimentation. A few keys to successful gluten-free slow cooking are essential to master: the type of thickener used (see "Gluten-Free Slow Cooking Staples" on page 19), the cooking time and temperature, the amount of liquid used, and the shape and volume of the ingredients. Once you have a firm grasp on these essentials, you'll be able to successfully convert favorite recipes to slow cooking in no time. Keep in mind that slow cooking is very forgiving. Here are a few tips for adapting recipes for slow cooking:

Find a similar recipe. Look through this book to see if you can find a recipe like the one you would like to adapt. For example, if you'd like to make your favorite seafood chowder in a slow cooker, compare it to our Seafood Chowder (page 66). Look at the two recipes side by side and come up with a recipe plan that combines the two. If you plan and write down a recipe before you head into the kitchen to experiment, the results are more likely to be successful.

Precook ground meats and fresh mushrooms. With a few exceptions (meatloaf, meatballs, and stuffed peppers, for example), we find that both the taste and appearance of the final dish is vastly improved if you cook whatever ground meat you intend to use *before* you put it in the slow cooker. You can brown large cuts of meat as well, a process that adds a layer of flavor to the dish and draws out some of the fat (which you can then discard). Raw mushrooms are another ingredient that benefits from precooking because they tend to release a large amount of liquid while they're cooking—which can affect the consistency of the final dish. When in doubt, precook mushrooms just as you would ground meats. Of course, there is always an exception to every rule—even in our book! In a few recipes, such as Beef Stroganoff (page 146) and Steak Diane Pot Roast (page 153), we intentionally do not precook the mushrooms because we want the mushroom liquid to enhance the sauce. Another option is to use canned mushrooms (though we prefer the fresh ones).

Remove poultry skin before cooking. Skinless poultry looks better and is certainly more healthful than poultry with the skin left on. The fat released by the skin into a mixed dish containing poultry can adversely affect the overall recipe. Conveniently, skinned poultry parts are available in most supermarkets, or you can easily remove the skin at home.

The exception to this rule is turkey breasts or whole chickens—it's much easier to pull the skin off after cooking and before eating, instead of removing the skin before slow cooking. Remember, the wet cooking environment of your slow cooker will keep poultry moist and juicy, even if it's skinless.

Cut the amount of liquid in half except for soups. If you're converting a stove-top recipe for the slow cooker, you'll need to drastically reduce the amount of liquid added during cooking because there is no evaporative loss in slow cooking. Also, meats and most vegetables release a fair amount of liquid when cooked.

Place root vegetables in the bottom of the slow cooker. Root vegetables such as potatoes and carrots take longer to cook than other vegetables, so they do better when placed on the bottom or along the sides of the slow cooker, where they receive the most heat. If you're going to layer ingredients, put these vegetables on the bottom layer. Also, be sure to cut ingredients (vegetables especially) into uniform sizes so they cook evenly. Having big chunks of carrot and small cubes of everything else in a soup, for example, means that the carrot pieces will not be thoroughly cooked when the other ingredients are done—not ideal! For a couple of examples in this book, check out Mimi's Classic Pork Roast (page 137) and Butter Bean Stew (page 92).

Add dairy products at the end of cooking. Milk proteins separate if cooked for a long time. While this will not affect the taste of the finished product, it will affect the texture and presentation. Nobody wants to eat what looks like curdled milk.

Let the slow cooker work for you! Stews, beans, and pot roasts love long, slow cooking (8 to 10 hours on LOW). Roasted nuts, seafood, eggs, and puddings favor shorter cook times, but the fear of overcooking or burning something is diminished with slow cooking. As a general rule, recipes tend to do better on LOW heat when cooked in a slow cooker. Certainly most foods can easily be cooked on HIGH (and we've indicated the few in our book that cannot), but we feel that the real joy of slow cooking is actually *cooking slowly*. There's satisfaction in putting food in the slow cooker in the morning, knowing that when you arrive home at night you'll be greeted by enticing aromas as soon as you open the door and that dinner will be cooked, tender, and ready to eat.

Modifying Gluten-Containing Slow Cooker Recipes for Gluten-Free Eating

If you're new to the gluten-free lifestyle or if you're craving the flavor of a favorite gluten-containing slow-cooker recipe, you may not feel confident about modifying it—not only for the slow cooker, but also so that it doesn't contain gluten. It's a rather tall order, we realize. That's why we've pulled together some basic instructions and tips about how to switch out gluten-containing ingredients in regular slow cooker recipes.

The first possibility is to substitute a grain without gluten. In a typical beef and barley slow cooker recipe, for example, brown rice, quinoa, and lentils are wonderful substitutes for the barley. Swapping a safe gluten-free grain for the barley is easy and effective. If you are new to cooking with whole grains, brown rice might be your best bet as you transition to gluten-free cooking. Medium-grain brown rice is an appropriate swap for barley because it is similar in shape and texture. Keep in mind that you can substitute grains in equal portions, but the amount of liquid needed might vary slightly from grain to grain (see the chart below for amounts of liquid needed for cooking single grains). Slow cooking should be low stress, and in general the recipes are very forgiving. If you add too much liquid, the grains will cook just fine; you'll simply end up with more cooking juices. And while we're talking beef and barley, check out our recipe for Beef with Lentils and Mushrooms (page 144). We don't think you'll miss the barley a bit!

Another possibility is to slow cook the protein and add precooked gluten-free grain later. Sometimes all you're really looking for in a slow cooker recipe is tender, flavorful meat, right? That is what the slow cooker does best, after all. Using our beef and barley example, you could actually leave the grain out of the recipe completely and just slow cook the meat and vegetables. When the meat is done cooking and you've thickened the cooking liquid (if desired), you can simply stir in a gluten-free grain that you've precooked. If you're using a grain that you batch-cooked days before and then refrigerated (or even froze), simply bring it back to life by adding a couple of tablespoons of water and microwaving it. Adding the warm grain to the hot, slow-cooked protein means dinner is ready. (We don't recommend adding a cold precooked grain to the heated protein—it can shock the slow cooker and lead to cracking. It also means you'll have to wait quite a while until the slow cooker brings the entire mixture back up to serving temperature.)

Slow Cooking Single Grains

If you want to use your slow cooker to cook gluten-free grains, legumes, and seeds perfectly, here are our cooking recommendations. In general, we like to cook grains on HIGH because it preserves more of their distinctive texture. If that's not important to you, feel free to cook any of the items we've listed for double the recommended time on the LOW setting. (Another exception is using the LOW setting for grains to be used in a breakfast cereal mixture where you want a creamy texture).

Single-Grain Slow-Cooking Guide

Cook 1 cup of the following items in the slow cooker on HIGH.

GRAIN	AMOUNT OF LIQUID	TIME	YIELD
AMARANTH	2½ cups water or broth	2 hours	2½ cups
BUCKWHEAT (*also known as kasha and groats*)	2 cups water or broth	2 hours	2½ cups
LENTILS	1½ cups water or broth	2 hours	2 cups
MILLET	2¾ cups water or broth	2 hours	3½ cups
OATS, steel-cut*	3 cups water	3–4 hours	3 cups
PEAS (*split*)	2 cups water or broth	2 hours	2¼ cups
QUINOA	1¾ cups water or broth	2–3 hours	3½ cups
RICE, BROWN	2¼ cups water or broth	3 hours	2 cups
RICE, WHITE	2 cups water or broth	2½ hours	2 cups

* Use only certified gluten-free oats. Steel-cut oats (also called Irish oatmeal) for oatmeal breakfast cereal can be cooked on LOW for 6 to 8 hours. When done, stir in 1 additional cup of water, milk, or soy milk.

Slow Cooking
Dried Beans

Dried beans cannot be added directly to a slow cooker recipe without being hydrated. We use two methods to hydrate beans for slow cooker recipes: precooking the beans or soaking them. The precooking method is used when there is an acid present in the recipe, such as vinegar in baked beans. Soaking dried beans is required for nonacidic recipes such as soups.

To precook dried beans: Rinse and pick through the beans. Add them to your slow cooker crock and cover with at least two inches of water. Cover the crock and cook the beans for 8 hours on LOW (perfect for overnight cooking), then drain.

To soak dried beans overnight: This is the classic method for hydrating beans. Rinse and pick through beans. Place in a pot, cover with two inches of water, cover the pot, and soak overnight.

To quick-soak dried beans: Rinse the beans in a fine mesh strainer. Place the beans in a large pot. Cover them with at least two inches of water and bring to a boil over high heat. Boil the beans for ten minutes and then remove from the heat. Cover the pot and let the beans sit for one hour, then drain.

Note: PRECOOKED BEANS can be used any way you would use canned beans. You can also freeze them for future use. Beans that are SOAKED OVERNIGHT or QUICK-SOAKED need further cooking.

MEASUREMENT EQUIVALENTS

dash or pinch	=	less than ⅛ teaspoon
3 teaspoons	=	1 tablespoon
4 tablespoons	=	¼ cup
16 tablespoons	=	1 cup
2 cups	=	1 pint
2 pints	=	1 quart
4 quarts	=	1 gallon
1 fluid ounce	=	2 tablespoons
8 fluid ounces	=	1 cup
16 ounces	=	1 pound

METRIC CONVERSIONS

WEIGHT

1 ounce	=	30 grams
1 pound	=	450 grams
2.2 pounds	=	1 kilogram

VOLUME / LIQUID

1 teaspoon	=	5 milliliters		
1 tablespoon	=	15 milliliters		
1 cup	=	250 milliliters		
1 quart	=	1000 milliliters	=	1 liter

4

The Gluten-Free Pantry

Stocking your home kitchen with gluten-free essentials for cooking (and eating) isn't exactly difficult, but it will undoubtedly take some time—especially in the beginning. It is, however, essential for successfully living a gluten-free lifestyle. Having staple items handy at home means that you won't get stuck with nothing suitable to eat. You'll be less likely to take dietary risks with foods that might not be gluten-free, and you'll feel confident and empowered in the kitchen, instead of frustrated and desperate! Here we provide some ideas to make your shopping trips more efficient, and we share some of our favorite gluten-free ingredients, brands, and manufacturers.

Where to Find Gluten-Free Foods

Just a few years ago, it could be tricky to find special, gluten-free foods, but that simply isn't the case any longer. Health food stores and food co-ops are still good options for gluten-free ingredients and prepared foods. Online retailers of gluten-free foods are easy to find now, too, and some offer a vast array of products and brands. Here are a few of our favorite gluten-free "supermarket" sites:

The Gluten-Free Mall: www.glutenfreemall.com
Glutenfree.com: www.glutenfree.com
Gluten-Free Trading Company: www.food4celiacs.com

In addition, a growing number of food manufacturers are selling gluten-free foods directly to individuals via the Internet. If one of your favorite brands is especially hard to come by locally, check out the manufacturer's site online and see if it's possible to order the product directly from the company. You will need to store the product, since most items are only available by the case, so be sure you use it often enough to make it worth devoting storage space. Don't expect online orders to always be less expensive than purchasing the same products from the supermarket. Sometimes you can get a great deal, sometimes not, and don't forget to add the cost of shipping to the overall cost of the food.

Perhaps the most convenient of all locations, however, is the good old neighborhood supermarket. If you haven't checked out the "health food aisle" lately, you may be surprised at just how many gluten-free foods are in stock now. Indeed, some of the larger grocery stores even have entire "gluten-free sections," which make shopping much more efficient. The sight of shelves full of "safe" foods surely is a long-awaited pleasure for the gluten-free shopper.

Shopping Strategies

Here are some ideas to help you be a more efficient shopper while also playing it safe with gluten.

1. Build your diet around foods that are naturally gluten-free. This not only makes it easier to eat safely, but is more healthful than filling your diet with a plethora of processed foods. You'll get more nutrition for your money if you stick mostly with produce, lean protein, and legumes, adding eggs and dairy if you tolerate them.

2. Get in the habit of using a shopping list. A handwritten list is fine, but you can save yourself some time by making up a list of staple items (including brands if you like) and keeping it on your computer, and then printing it out and checking off the items you need for each shopping trip. Or keep a running list of items you need on your smartphone. However you choose to do it, using a list will help you be more efficient (no more wandering around the supermarket aisles trying to remember what you need). It may also prevent you from overspending

A Label-Reading Reminder

Anyone who has been eating gluten-free for a while will tell you that a "better safe than sorry" approach to purchasing processed foods is necessary. That means that even if the food was gluten-free the last time you purchased it, you should check the ingredient list each and every time you purchase it. Not sure about something you see? Call the manufacturer, and be specific about the information you're seeking.

and loading up on impulse-purchase treats that are usually less than healthy.

3. Join with other people who need gluten-free foods and combine your online shopping orders. You'll save money buying in bulk and splitting the shipping costs.

4. Obtain a list of gluten-free items and brands that are available at your favorite market. Many stores supply these lists at the customer service desk, as well as on their website.

5. Do not purchase food items from bulk bins, even if the foods are generally considered gluten-free. The chances of cross-contamination are great—it's just too risky.

6. Once you get your purchases home, be sure to label and store them properly to avoid cross-contamination (see "Keeping Your Gluten-Free Food Safe to Eat" on page 9).

Selected Brands of Gluten-Free Products

While developing the recipes in this book, we relied on a number of gluten-free ingredients time and time again. In fact, you'll see these brands noted in ingredient lists where appropriate. By no means could we ever include a list of *all* the gluten-free products currently available. More and more products reach the market every day, while others fade away. However, we thought you might like to investigate the products we used—hence this listing. Finally, we included information on a few other gluten-free products we've encountered—just because we like them!

BAKING MIXES
AND ALTERNATIVE FLOURS

Betty Crocker gluten-free baking mixes
    www.bettycrocker.com
Bisquick Gluten-Free Baking Mix
    www.bettycrocker.com
Bob's Red Mill gluten-free products
    www.bobsredmill.com
Pamela's Products baking mixes
    www.pamelasproducts.com

BROTH AND BOUILLON

Better than Bouillon (organic)
    www.superiortouch.com
Kitchen Basics
    www.kitchenbasics.net
Pacific Natural Foods
    www.pacificfoods.com

CEREALS AND OATS

Bob's Red Mill gluten-free products
    www.bobsredmill.com
Chex cereals
    www.chex.com
Envirokids Gorilla Munch and other cereals
    www.naturespath.com
Erewhon cereals
    www.erewhonmarket.com

CHIPS, CRACKERS, AND COOKIES

Glenny's
    www.glennys.com
Mary's Gone Crackers
    www.marysgonecrackers.com
Pamela's Products
    www.pamelasproducts.com
Tostitos Scoops, Fritos Scoops
    www.fritolay.com

CONDIMENTS

Frank's Red Hot Sauce
    www.franksredhot.com
Grey Poupon Dijon Mustard
    http://brands.kraftfoods.com
Gulden's Spicy Brown Mustard
    www.conagrafoods.com
San-J Wheat-Free Tamari
    www.san-j.com
Tabasco
    www.tabasco.com
Thai Kitchen fish sauce, curry paste
    www.thaikitchen.com

GRAINS, COUSCOUS, AND PASTA

Lundberg brown rice, couscous, pastas
    www.lundberg.com
Trader Joe's brown rice, fusilli
    www.traderjoes.com
Uncle Ben's Ready Rice (Original)
    www.unclebens.com

MEAT PRODUCTS

Hormel bacon toppings, lunch meats
    www.hormel.com

MISCELLANEOUS

Amy's Kitchen canned chili
    www.amys.com
Bragg Liquid Aminos
    www.bragg.com
Classico Traditional Basil Pesto
    www.classico.com
Colgin Liquid Smoke
    www.colgin.com
Earth Balance Vegan Buttery Sticks
    www.earthbalancenatural.com
Luzianne Cajun Seasoning
    www.luzianne.com
Muir Glen tomato products, salsa
    www.muirglen.com
Solo almond paste
    www.solofoods.com

SAUCES, DRESSINGS, AND MARINADES

Gravy Master
    www.gravy.com
Ken's Buffalo Wing Sauce
    www.kensfoods.com
Ken's marinades, salad dressings
    www.kensfoods.com
Mrs. Richardson's Caramel Topping
    www.brfoods.com
Sweet Baby Ray's barbeque sauces
    www.kensfoods.com

TORTILLAS, PITAS, AND BREADS

Food for Life tortillas
    www.foodforlife.com
GFL Foods gluten-free pita bread
    www.gflfoods.com
Rose's Bakery gluten-free pita bread
    www.rosesbakery.com
Udi's gluten-free bread
    www.udisglutenfree.com

Breakfast and Brunch

Hot Brown Rice Cereal with Dried Fruits

Serves 8 (about ½ cup each)

Japanese medium-grain rice delivers a lovely, creamy breakfast cereal. If you can't locate it in your market, simply substitute another brown rice. Any leftover cereal can be frozen for future breakfasts—very handy for in-a-hurry mornings! The seasoning spice is your choice—classic cinnamon or exotic cardamom.

3¾ cups water

1 cup Japanese medium-grain brown rice

½ cup natural applesauce

¼ cup dried cranberries

¼ cup chopped dried apricots

2 tablespoons dried currants

2 tablespoons real maple syrup or honey

2 tablespoons butter

½ teaspoon ground cinnamon or ground cardamom

¼ teaspoon kosher salt

⅛ teaspoon ground ginger

toasted almonds or walnuts (optional)

light cream (optional)

1. Stir together all ingredients except nuts and cream in the slow cooker crock. Cover and cook 1 hour on LOW (or 30 minutes on HIGH). Stir, then cover and cook an additional 7 hours on LOW (or 3–3½ hours on HIGH).

2. Stir cereal well before serving. Garnish cereal with nuts and a touch of cream, if desired.

Dairy-Free Variation

Replace butter with canola oil.
Use soy milk in place of cream.

Maple and Brown Sugar Multigrain Breakfast Cereal

Serves 12 (about ½ cup each)

Instant oatmeal is not an option for most gluten-free folks. Kimberly came up with this recipe for her husband because he missed his old standard. She is quite proud of her sneaky, healthy addition of quinoa flakes and flax. Be sure to purchase certified gluten-free oats.

1. Stir together all ingredients except milk and bananas in the slow cooker crock. Cover and cook 8 hours on LOW (or 4 hours on HIGH).

2. Stir well before serving. If desired, garnish cereal with a little milk and some sliced bananas.

Dairy-Free Variation

Replace butter with canola oil.
Use soy milk in place of regular milk.

7 cups water
1¼ cups steel-cut oats
    (such as Bob's Red Mill®)
½ cup whole millet
½ cup quinoa flakes
⅓ cup real maple syrup
3 tablespoons light brown sugar
2 tablespoons butter
2 tablespoons golden flax meal
1 teaspoon vanilla extract
¼ teaspoon kosher salt
milk (optional)
sliced bananas (optional)

Overnight Irish Oatmeal with Nuts and Berries

Serves 12 (about ½ cup each)

Waking up to a warm bowl of oatmeal is a delicious (not to mention a super speedy) way to start the day. A little prep the night before can make it a reality. Be sure to use certified, gluten-free steel-cut oats.

6½ cups water

1½ cups steel-cut oats
    (such as Bob's Red Mill®)

¼ cup sugar (optional)

1 tablespoon butter

½ teaspoon vanilla extract

½ teaspoon kosher salt

1½ cup toasted walnuts, pecans,
    or almonds

6 cups fresh blueberries, strawberries,
    or raspberries

light cream (optional)

1. Stir together all ingredients except nuts, berries, and cream in the slow cooker crock. Cover and cook 8 hours on LOW (or 4 hours on HIGH).

2. Stir oatmeal well before serving. Garnish each portion of oatmeal with 2 generous tablespoons of nuts and ½ cup of berries. Drizzle a bit of light cream over the oatmeal, if desired.

Dairy-Free Variation

Replace butter with canola oil.
Use soy milk in place of cream.

INGREDIENT INFO Steel-cut oats, also called Scotch oats, Irish oats, or coarse-cut oats, are whole-grain oats that have been coarsely chopped. When cooked, they are toothsome and hearty. They are ideal for slow cooker preparation because their texture holds up during the long cooking time.

Seasonal Variations

Need a few ideas to make your morning bowl of oatmeal appropriate for the season? We've got a few suggestions to get you started:

SUMMER—substitute fresh **peach** slices or **plums** for the berries

WINTER—substitute sliced **bananas** or **mangoes** for the berries

FALL—substitute chopped **apples** or **pears** for the berries

Honeyed Millet Porridge

Serves 10 (about ½ cup each)

Millet is a tiny, gluten-free grain with a mild flavor and delicate bite. It can be prepared in both sweet and savory ways. We've opted for the former here to deliver a satisfying, simple breakfast cereal.

4 cups water
  (plus more if needed)
1½ cups whole-grain millet
¼ cup honey
2 tablespoons butter
¼ teaspoon kosher salt
chopped dried apricots (optional)
apricot jam (optional)

1. Stir together all ingredients except the apricots and jam in the slow cooker crock, making sure that the honey dissolves in the water. Cover and cook 7–8 hours on LOW (or 3½ hours on HIGH).

2. Stir in additional water to thin the porridge slightly, if needed. Garnish each bowl with a sprinkling of chopped dried apricots or some jam, if desired.

Dairy-Free Variation

Replace butter with canola oil.

INGREDIENT INFO   Though underutilized in the West, millet has been a staple grain for thousands of years in Africa and Asia. Millet is versatile, grows quickly, and can withstand a hot, arid environment, making it a valuable crop in places where other crops frequently fail.

Nut and Seed Granola

Serves 16 (about ¾ cup each)

This is serious, high-end granola that's enriched with protein-packed quinoa flakes. The best part, though, is the abundance of nuts and seeds (feel free to substitute different nuts according to your preference). Using a slow cooker for this recipe results in perfectly toasted granola—and there's no chance of its burning in the oven.

1. Whisk together the butter, honey, sesame seeds, brown sugar, vanilla, almond extract, cinnamon, and salt in the slow cooker crock.

2. Stir in the almonds, pumpkin seeds, sunflower seeds, quinoa flakes, and pecans, making sure that they all are coated with the honey mixture. Cover and cook 1 hour on HIGH.

3. Stir granola, then prop lid open with wooden spoon handle. Cook an additional 1½–2 hours on HIGH, stirring every 30 minutes or so. Continue to keep the lid vented during cooking. The granola is done when it becomes a toasted golden brown.

4. Transfer hot granola to a sheet pan lined with parchment paper or foil. Allow granola to cool completely. Break up the granola and store in an airtight container at room temperature for up to 2 weeks.

½ cup melted butter or canola oil

½ cup honey or real maple syrup

⅓ cup sesame seeds

¼ cup light brown sugar

2 teaspoons vanilla extract

¾ teaspoon almond extract

½ teaspoon ground cinnamon

½ teaspoon kosher salt

2½ cups sliced almonds

1½ cups raw pumpkin seeds

1½ cups raw sunflower seeds

1½ cups quinoa flakes

1 cup raw pecans or macadamia nuts

Dairy-Free Variation

Replace butter with canola oil.

INGREDIENT INFO Quinoa flakes are precooked, rolled quinoa. Look for them in the gluten-free section or alongside the hot breakfast cereals at your supermarket.

Almond Granola with Dates and Coconut

Serves 16 (½ cup each)

If you have ever let oven-baked granola go a minute too long and ended up with a charred mess, you will surely appreciate slow-cooked granola and its forgiving nature. This is a classic granola with ample nuts and fruit. The coconut, ginger, and nutmeg give it a bit of a Caribbean flair. Be sure to use certified gluten-free oats.

½ cup melted butter or canola oil

3 tablespoons brown sugar

3 tablespoons honey or maple syrup

1 teaspoon almond extract

¼ teaspoon kosher salt

½ teaspoon freshly grated nutmeg
    or ¼ teaspoon ground nutmeg

¼ teaspoon ground ginger

3 cups old-fashioned oats
    such as Bob's Red Mill®)

2 cups crispy brown rice cereal
    (such as Erewhon®)

1½ cups sliced almonds

1 cup unsweetened dried coconut flakes

2 tablespoons golden flax meal

1 cup chopped dates

1. Whisk together the butter, brown sugar, honey, almond extract, salt, nutmeg, and ginger in the slow cooker crock. Stir in the oats, rice cereal, almonds, coconut, and flax. Stir well to coat with the brown sugar mixture. Cover and cook 1 hour on HIGH.

2. Stir well and prop lid open with wooden spoon handle. Continue to cook on HIGH for an additional 1½–2 hours, stirring every 30 minutes or so. Continue to keep the lid vented during cooking. The granola is done when it becomes a toasted golden brown.

3. Add the dates to the granola and stir well to combine. Transfer hot granola to a sheet pan lined with parchment paper or foil. Allow granola to cool completely. Break up granola and store in an airtight container for up to 2 weeks.

Dairy-Free Variation

Replace butter with canola oil.

INGREDIENT INFO Sometimes chopped dates are processed with flour. Be sure to check the package label. If you cannot find any chopped dates that are gluten-free, purchase whole dates and chop them yourself.

Bacon, Onion, and Spinach Frittata

Serves 6 (about ¾ cup each)

The basic ingredients in a frittata are much like those in an omelet—eggs, vegetables, meat, cheese, etc.—but making a frittata is much easier than filling and folding an omelet, since all the ingredients are mixed together and cooked until they're firm. This bacon, onion, and spinach frittata makes a lovely brunch dish or a light supper served with a leafy salad.

1. Coat the slow cooker crock with cooking spray; set aside.

2. In a large mixing bowl, stir together all ingredients, reserving half the shredded cheese for topping. Add the mixture to the crock, spreading it evenly to the edges.

3. Cover and cook 2½ hours on LOW. Sprinkle the top of the frittata with the remaining cheese, then cover and cook an additional ½ hour until frittata is set and cheese topping is melted. Do not overcook or the frittata will be dry.

Nonstick cooking spray

6 eggs, beaten

1 (10-ounce) package frozen, chopped spinach, thawed and squeezed dry

1 (8-ounce) package shredded Colby-Jack cheese, divided

1 (2.8-ounce) package cooked bacon pieces, or 8 slices cooked and crumbled bacon

¾ cup chopped scallions (5 or 6 whole scallions)

2 tablespoons half-and-half

1 teaspoon minced garlic

½ teaspoon kosher salt

¼ teaspoon ground black pepper

Spanish Tortilla

Serves 6

After developing Migas Casserole (see page 43) for the slow cooker—using tortilla chips—Kimberly adapted this recipe for one of Spain's most beloved dishes using potato chips instead of potatoes. In fact, the Spanish "tortilla" has nothing to do with tortillas at all. Rather, it is a thin omelet filled with potatoes. The experiment worked, and though our version, which is embellished with prosciutto and roasted red peppers, isn't exactly authentic, we think you'll find the results most delicious! Serve Spanish Tortilla warm or at room temperature.

Nonstick cooking spray

2½ cups purchased kettle-cooked potato chips

8 eggs

¼ cup water

⅓ cup finely chopped roasted red peppers

⅓ cup finely chopped prosciutto di Parma

2 scallions, thinly sliced

¼ teaspoon kosher salt

¼ teaspoon ground black pepper

pinch cayenne pepper

1. Coat the inside of the slow cooker crock with cooking spray. Line the bottom of the crock with an even layer of the chips; set aside.

2. Whisk together the eggs and water in a medium mixing bowl. Add the remaining ingredients and stir well to combine.

3. Pour the egg mixture over the chips. Use a spoon to very gently mix the eggs and chips (it is okay if the chips stick out of the top of the mixture).

4. Cover and cook 4 hours on LOW (or 1½ hours on HIGH). The center of the tortilla should be set. Let the tortilla rest, uncovered, 10 minutes. Run a knife around the edge of the tortilla before cutting in wedges.

Tex-Mex Egg Bake (Migas Casserole)

Serves 6

Migas is a classic Tex-Mex dish that makes good use of stale tortillas. We've streamlined the process a bit by using store-bought tortilla chips. This dish makes a wonderful brunch offering and would also be perfect for a weekend supper with black beans and rice.

1. Coat the slow cooker crock with cooking spray; set aside.

2. Whisk the eggs briefly in a medium mixing bowl. Stir in the half-and-half, scallions, green chilies, cheeses, and pepper until mixture is blended. Add the tortilla chips and stir, breaking up any large chips. Transfer the mixture to the crock (the chips will float to the top and some will stick out of the mixture; this is okay).

3. Cover and cook 2½–3 hours on LOW (or 1½ hours on HIGH). The casserole is done when the center is cooked through. Let the egg bake rest, uncovered, for 10 minutes before cutting into wedges.

4. Top each portion with salsa, avocado, and cilantro.

Nonstick cooking spray

8 eggs

⅔ cup half-and-half

3 scallions, thinly sliced

1 (4-ounce) can green chilies

1 cup shredded pepper-jack cheese

1 cup shredded cheddar cheese

¼ teaspoon ground black pepper

3 cups corn tortilla chips
    (such as Tostitos®)

1 cup salsa (such as Muir Glen®)

1 avocado, chopped

⅓ cup finely chopped cilantro

Cheesy Cheddar and Ham Bake

Serves 10 (about 1 cup each)

This hearty dish can be paired with berries for brunch or a green salad for supper. The shorter than normal cooking time makes this recipe an ideal candidate for weekend slow cooking.

Nonstick cooking spray

3 cups frozen shredded hash browns, thawed

2 cups ricotta cheese

1½ cups shredded sharp cheddar cheese

¾ cup shredded Swiss cheese

6 eggs, beaten

½ pound cooked deli ham (such as Hormel Natural Choice®), chopped

1 teaspoon Tabasco® or more to taste

½ teaspoon kosher salt

¼ teaspoon ground black pepper

1. Coat the inside of the slow cooker crock with cooking spray and set aside.

2. Stir together all remaining ingredients in a large mixing bowl until evenly blended. Transfer mixture to the slow cooker crock, spreading it evenly to the edges.

3. Cover and cook 5–6 hours on LOW (or 2½–3 hours on HIGH). The casserole will brown slightly on the edges and the center will be cooked through. Allow casserole to rest, uncovered, for 10 minutes before serving.

Maple Apple Slices

Serves 12 (about ½ cup each)

Cooked apples are such a delicious item to have on hand for topping oatmeal or yogurt. Of course, we would not suggest ice cream for breakfast, but these apples are divine over vanilla ice cream . . .

1. Stir together all ingredients in the slow cooker crock. Cover and cook 4 hours on LOW (or 2 hours on HIGH).

2. Stir well. Serve warm, or transfer apples to a separate container and refrigerate until needed.

2 tablespoons quick-cooking tapioca

3 pounds Granny Smith apples, peeled, cored, and thickly sliced

1¾ cups apple cider or apple juice

⅓ cup real maple syrup

½ teaspoon vanilla extract

¼ teaspoon kosher salt

INGREDIENT INFO   We like Granny Smith apples in this recipe because they are tart and hold their shape well during cooking. Feel free to substitute your favorite apple, but be aware that softer varieties have a tendency to cook down to the consistency of applesauce in a slow cooker.

Jammy Berry Sauce

Serves 16 (about ¼ cup each)

This versatile, jam-like sauce makes a luscious topping for gluten-free French toast, hot cereal, cottage cheese, or yogurt. It's also suitable as a dessert topping and is tasty when eaten chilled or warmed. Feel free to vary the berry mixture to your liking—we like a frozen berry mix that includes blackberries (but some might object to the seeds).

DAIRY-FREE

7 cups frozen, unsweetened mixed berries, thawed

½ cup light brown sugar

2 tablespoons quick-cooking tapioca

2 tablespoons water

¼ teaspoon ground cinnamon

½ cup water

1. Stir together berries, brown sugar, tapioca, 2 tablespoons water, and cinnamon in the slow cooker crock. Cover and cook 3 hours on LOW.

2. Stir in ½ cup water, adding more if necessary to reach desired consistency. (Refrigerate any unused sauce in a covered container for up to 3 weeks.)

TECHNIQUE TIP   If you prefer a smooth sauce or syrup, puree the sauce in a blender (or use an immersion blender) after cooking; then add water to reach the desired consistency.

Apple Butter

Makes 3½ cups

Not sure what to do with all the apples from apple picking? We can't think of a better way to use those apples than to make sweet, thick apple butter. Stir it into hot cereal for a change of pace, or serve it with pork chops.

1. Stir together all ingredients in the slow cooker crock. Cover and cook 4 hours on HIGH.

2. Stir well. Use an immersion blender to process the apple butter until smooth. Alternatively, the apple butter can be processed in a blender or food processor (be careful, it's very hot) and returned to the slow cooker crock.

3. Prop lid open with a wooden spoon and cook another 2 hours on HIGH. Remove lid and allow apple butter to cool in the crock.

4. Transfer apple butter to containers and refrigerate up to 1 month (or can or freeze).

8 cups peeled, chopped apples (about 3 pounds; we use McIntosh)

¾ cup sugar

¼ cup brown sugar

1 tablespoon lemon juice

1¼ teaspoon cinnamon

¼ teaspoon kosher salt

¼ teaspoon freshly grated nutmeg or ⅛ teaspoon ground nutmeg

⅛ teaspoon ground cloves

TECHNIQUE TIP Using an immersion blender, or stick blender, makes it easy to puree ingredients right in the cooking pot—there's no need to transfer hot food to a blender and back, risking messy (not to mention painfully hot) splatters. These handy little appliances are moderately priced and often go on special sale around the holidays.

Pumpkin Butter

Makes about 4 cups

What can you do with pumpkin butter? Kimberly's husband enjoys it on crispy rice crackers over a thin layer of whipped cream cheese. You can also swirl it into espresso and steamed milk for a delicious pumpkin latte. Mix it into hot cereal, stir it into yogurt, or just top your favorite gluten-free toast with this luscious spread. This recipe for pumpkin butter makes quite a bit, so give some to your neighbors and friends!

1 (29-ounce) can pumpkin puree (**not** pumpkin pie filling)

¾ cup white sugar

½ cup packed brown sugar

⅓ cup real maple syrup or honey

¼ cup apple cider or apple juice

1 tablespoon lemon juice

1 tablespoon grated fresh ginger or 1½ teaspoons ground ginger

1½ teaspoon cinnamon

¾ teaspoon freshly grated nutmeg or ½ teaspoon ground nutmeg

⅛ teaspoon ground cloves

⅛ teaspoon kosher salt

1. Stir together all ingredients in the slow cooker crock. Cover and cook 1 hour on HIGH.

2. Stir well, then prop the lid open with wooden spoon handle. Cook an additional 1–2 hours on HIGH, stirring every 30 minutes or so. Continue to keep the lid vented during cooking. The pumpkin butter is done when all the liquid has been absorbed into the pumpkin and the mixture looks smooth. It will darken slightly.

3. Remove lid and allow the pumpkin butter to cool in the slow cooker. Divide between small jars or freezer jam containers. Refrigerate or freeze. If freezing, be sure to leave at least ½-inch of headroom because the pumpkin butter will expand slightly as it freezes.

Appetizers and Snacks

6

Recipe Variation
DAIRY-FREE

Easy Taco Dip

Serves 14 (about ½ cup each)

Really, what's a party without a Tex-Mex-inspired dip? Ours was developed using a two-quart slow cooker, but it could easily be made in a larger crock (and also doubled or tripled if you like). Serve this with gluten-free tortilla chips—then stand back from the crowd!

2 (16-ounce) cans refried beans

1 (14.7-ounce) can chili with beans (such as Amy's Organic® Black Bean Chili)

1 (4-ounce) can diced green chilies

1½ teaspoons GF Chili Powder (page 200)

For the topping

1 (8-ounce) package cream cheese, softened

½ cup sour cream

1 large tomato, chopped

1 ripe avocado, peeled, pitted, and chopped

½ cup shredded sharp cheddar cheese

½ cup chopped scallions

1. Stir together the refried beans, chili, diced chilies, and chili powder in a large mixing bowl. Transfer mixture to the slow cooker crock. Cover and cook 1½ hours on LOW.

2. Stir together the cream cheese and sour cream in a small bowl. Spoon the cream cheese and sour cream mixture over the beans and chili mixture. Cover and switch slow cooker to WARM setting for 15–30 minutes, until cream cheese mixture is warmed and melted.

3. Top dip with the tomatoes and avocados, then the cheese. Sprinkle the top with the scallions.

Spinach-Artichoke Dip

Serves 12 (about ⅓ cup each)

This homemade version of a restaurant favorite couldn't be easier. Serve it with raw veggies and your favorite gluten-free crackers.

1. Stir together all ingredients except mozzarella in the slow cooker crock. Cover and cook 1½ hours on LOW.

2. Sprinkle mozzarella over top of dip. Cover and cook an additional ½ hour until mozzarella is melted. To serve, switch slow cooker to WARM setting.

12 ounces reduced-fat cream cheese, softened (also called Neufchâtel cheese)

1 cup shredded Parmesan-Romano cheese blend (or ½ cup of each)

¾ cup light mayonnaise (such as Hellmann's Light®)

1 (10-ounce) package frozen chopped spinach, thawed and squeezed dry

1 (9-ounce) package frozen artichoke hearts, thawed

½ cup finely chopped red bell pepper

2 teaspoons minced garlic

¼ teaspoon garlic salt

¼ teaspoon Tabasco®

1 cup shredded part-skim mozzarella cheese

Bacon, Scallion, and Cheddar Dip

Serves 20 (about ¼ cup each)

Warm, cheesy dips are a perennial party-time favorite, and this one is bound to please the guests at your next soiree. Sharp cheddar melted with cream cheese and mixed with a generous amount of bacon and scallions—what's not to like? Serve it with chunks of your favorite gluten-free bread or crackers. As slow cooker recipes go, this is quick cooking—only 1½ hours and it's done, but if you switch your slow cooker down to the warm setting, your guests can enjoy it for a few hours . . . if it lasts that long. . . .

2 (8-ounce) packages shredded, sharp cheddar cheese

1 (8-ounce) package cream cheese, softened

1 (8-ounce) tub "chive and onion" cream cheese spread

1½ cups half-and-half

1 teaspoon dry mustard

½ teaspoon Tabasco®

½ teaspoon minced garlic

¾ cup chopped scallions (5 or 6 scallions)

1 (2.8-ounce) package cooked bacon pieces (such as Oscar-Mayer®), or 8 slices bacon, cooked crisp and crumbled

1. Stir together all ingredients except scallions and bacon in the slow cooker crock. Cover and cook 1 hour on LOW.

2. Stir in the bacon pieces and scallions. Cover and cook an additional ½ hour. To serve, switch slow cooker to WARM setting.

Classic Cheddar Cheese Dip

Serves 16 (about ¼ cup each)

Nothing says "Party Time!" like warm cheese dip. Gluten-free pretzels are great dippers, but also consider sliced kielbasa, blanched broccoli, or steamed, bite-sized potatoes for dipping.

1. Stir together all ingredients except milk and Tabasco® in the slow cooker crock. Cover and cook 1 hour on LOW.

2. Stir in the milk and Tabasco®. Cover and cook an additional ½ hour. All the cheese should be melted and the dip should be very creamy. To serve, switch slow cooker to WARM setting. If the dip gets too thick during service, thin it with 2–3 tablespoons of milk.

1 (8-ounce) package shredded sharp cheddar cheese

1 (8-ounce) package shredded Monterey Jack cheese

1 (8-ounce) package cream cheese, at room temperature

1 cup sour cream

¾ cup milk

¼ teaspoon Tabasco® or more to taste

Variations

Mexican Queso Dip

Stir 1 (4-ounce) can diced **green chilies** and G teaspoon **GF Chili Powder** (page 200) into the cheese mixture. Serve with gluten-free corn chips (such as Tostitos®).

Beer and Cheese Dip

Replace milk with **gluten-free beer** (such as Redbridge® from Anheuser-Busch). The mixture will bubble up when the beer is added, but will settle as it cooks for the remaining half hour.

Louisiana Crab and Pecan Dip

Serves 10 (about ¼ cup each)

Blue crab is eaten in many forms in Louisiana, and many a home cook has a special crab dip recipe. Our version of this delicious dip substitutes gluten-free Bragg Liquid Aminos for the more traditional Worcestershire sauce. This recipe is best suited to a two-quart (or even a dip-sized) slow cooker, but if you've got a crowd, just double it and use a larger slow cooker. Serve the dip with your favorite gluten-free crackers.

1 (8-ounce) package cream cheese, softened

6 ounces fresh crab meat, picked over (or canned crabmeat, drained and flaked)

¼ cup plus 2 tablespoons chopped pecans, toasted

2 teaspoons dehydrated minced onion

1 teaspoon Bragg Liquid Aminos®

1 teaspoon horseradish or to taste (optional)

¼ teaspoon paprika

⅛ teaspoon celery seed

⅛ teaspoon Tabasco® (optional)

pinch cayenne pepper

1. Stir together all ingredients except 2 tablespoons chopped pecans in the slow cooker crock. Spread mixture in an even layer. Cover and cook 1½ hours on LOW.

2. Sprinkle top of dip with the reserved pecans. To serve, switch slow cooker to WARM setting.

Mary's Layered Buffalo Chicken Dip

Serves 14 (about ⅓ cup each)

Kimberly's friend, Mary Galarraga, often cooks gluten-free dishes because her mom has celiac disease. When Mary served this dip at a summer party, Kimberly asked for the recipe even before she knew it was gluten-free! It is classic party fare—creamy, cheesy, and easy. There are many versions of Buffalo chicken dip around; we really prefer the layered effect of this version.

1. Spread the cream cheese in an even layer in the bottom of the slow cooker crock. Add a layer of chicken, dressing, and hot sauce.

2. Cover and cook 1½ hours on LOW. Sprinkle the cheese over the dip. Cover and cook an additional 30 minutes until cheese is melted.

3. Top dip with scallions, if desired. To serve, switch slow cooker to WARM setting. Serve dip with corn chips and celery sticks.

INGREDIENT INFO The cooked rotisserie chickens sold at Whole Foods Market® are gluten-free. To save time cooking the chicken, you could certainly pull the breast meat from one of these chickens.

2 (8-ounce) containers soft cream cheese

3 cups bite-sized cooked chicken breast meat (about 1¼ pounds raw chicken)

1 (8-ounce) bottle blue cheese or ranch dressing (such as Ken's®)

1 cup bottled hot sauce (such as Frank's®)

1 cup shredded Monterey Jack or cheddar cheese

2 scallions, chopped (optional)

tortilla corn chips (such as Tostitos® Scoops)

celery sticks

Crunchy Parmesan Party Mix

Serves 22 (about ½ cup each)

Are you worried about the lack of gluten-free fare at your next cocktail party or school event? We suggest you bring this party mix along. Come to think of it, you may want to make an extra batch because *everyone* will happily dig into this savory treat.

1 stick butter

1¼ teaspoons garlic powder

1 teaspoon kosher salt

¼ teaspoon paprika

pinch ground cayenne pepper

4 cups Rice Chex® cereal

4 cups Corn Chex® cereal

2 cups Gorilla Munch® cereal
   (gluten-free crispy corn puffs)

1 (12-ounce) container roasted
   mixed nuts

¾ grated Parmesan cheese

1. Add the butter to a microwave-safe bowl. Heat for 45 seconds on low power, or until melted. Whisk in the garlic powder, kosher salt, paprika, and cayenne; set aside.

2. Stir the cereals and nuts together in the slow cooker crock. Whisk the butter mixture once more, then pour it over the cereal mixture, scraping any remaining seasonings onto the cereal.

3. Stir the cereal mixture until it is evenly coated with the butter and seasonings. Sprinkle the Parmesan over the cereal and stir well.

4. Cover and cook 1 hour on HIGH. Stir well. Prop lid open with a wooden spoon and cook another 40 minutes.

5. Transfer the cereal mix to a parchment lined baking sheet and allow it to cool completely. Transfer to a sealed container and store for up to 2 weeks at room temperature.

INGREDIENT INFO Gluten-free cereals can be found in several sections of the supermarket. Check the regular cereal aisle for old standards, like the General Mills Chex cereals we use in this recipe, and also check the health food aisle as well as the gluten-free section. As always, read those labels!

Barbecue Almonds

Serves 14 (about ¼ cup each)

Buttery, spicy, and salty, these almonds practically beg for ice-cold, gluten-free beer.

1. Place almonds in the slow cooker. Drizzle the butter over the almonds and stir to completely coat the nuts with butter. Stir in 2 tablespoons of the barbecue seasoning until nuts are well coated with seasoning. Cover and cook 2 hours on LOW, stirring several times during cooking.

2. Turn the slow cooker off and let the almonds cool completely in the slow cooker. When cool, stir in the remaining ½ teaspoon barbecue seasoning and the kosher salt. Transfer nuts to serving bowl or store in a covered container at room temperature for up to 2 weeks.

1 pound raw, whole almonds

2 tablespoons melted butter

2 tablespoons plus ½ teaspoon GF Barbecue Seasoning (page 201)

½ teaspoon kosher salt

Dairy-Free Variation

Replace butter with canola oil.

Indian Spiced Cashews

Serves 14 (about ¼ cup each)

The biggest cashews are usually more readily available around holiday time—a perfect time to roast a batch or two of these spicy-sweet nuts for gifts or get-togethers. Mixed nuts would be a good substitution. Be sure to check the label of the curry powder you use; most curry powders are gluten-free but it never hurts to check the labels on spice mixtures.

1 pound roasted and salted cashews

2 tablespoons melted butter

2 teaspoons sugar

1 teaspoon curry powder

¼ teaspoon cayenne pepper

¼ teaspoon cumin

¼ teaspoon ground coriander

⅛ teaspoon cinnamon

1. Place cashews in the slow cooker and set aside.

2. Stir together the remaining ingredients in a small bowl. Drizzle the mixture over the nuts and stir to completely coat the nuts with the butter mixture. Cover and cook 1½ hours on LOW, stirring several times during cooking.

3. Turn the slow cooker off and let the nuts cool completely in the slow cooker (about 2 hours). Transfer nuts to serving bowl or store in a covered container at room temperature for up to 2 weeks.

Dairy-Free Variation

Replace butter with canola oil.

INGREDIENT INFO Cashew nuts are the seeds of the cashew apple, the fruit of the cashew tree, which is native to the coastal areas of northeastern Brazil. Cashews come from several different countries. Brazilian cashews are generally the largest in size, and the softest. Indian cashews are smaller, but crunchier. Whatever type your store carries is fine for this recipe.

Chipotle-Lime Mixed Nuts

DAIRY-FREE

Serves 16 (about ¼ cup each)

Snack foods can be tricky in the land of gluten-free, which is why we love keeping a variety of nuts on hand—they're nutritious, delicious, and versatile. Just make sure you watch the portion size—jazzed-up nuts like these can be addictive! Oh, and don't forget that spiced nuts make a great gluten-free gift—for the hostess, the teacher, the dog-walker . . .

1. Whisk together the sugar, chipotle, 1 tablespoon of the lime zest, paprika, salt, cumin, and cayenne pepper in a medium bowl; set aside.

2. In a separate bowl, whisk the egg white until frothy. Add the nuts to the egg white. Toss well until the nuts are evenly coated with egg white. Transfer the nuts to the bowl with the spices and toss until they are well coated with the spices.

3. Transfer the coated nuts to the slow cooker crock. Cover and cook 1 hour on HIGH. Stir well. Prop lid open with a wooden spoon and cook another 45 minutes.

4. Transfer nuts to a parchment-lined baking sheet and allow them to cool completely. Toss the nuts with remaining teaspoon of lime zest. Transfer to a sealed container and store for up to 2 weeks at room temperature.

3 tablespoons sugar

1 tablespoon ground chipotle

1 tablespoon plus 1 teaspoon firmly packed lime zest, divided

½ teaspoon paprika (smoked or sweet)

½ teaspoon kosher salt

½ teaspoon ground cumin

pinch ground cayenne pepper or more to taste

1 egg white

1 pound roasted, salted deluxe mixed nuts

Mild Variation

We love this spicy blend of nuts, but if you prefer a milder blend, reduce the amount of chipotle to 2 teaspoons, the paprika to ¼ teaspoon, the cumin to ¼ teaspoon, and omit the cayenne pepper.

Sweet and Sour Kielbasa

Serves 12 (about ½ cup each)

DAIRY-
FREE

This easy, party-worthy appetizer also works as a family-friendly entrée when served over rice. Regular kielbasa can be substituted for the "lite" variety, but don't use turkey kielbasa—it gets tough in this dish.

1½ cups ketchup (such as Heinz®
 or Annie's Naturals®)

1 green pepper, finely chopped

1 red pepper, finely chopped

1 medium onion, thinly sliced

1 (8-ounce) can crushed pineapple
 (do not drain)

¼ cup brown sugar

3 tablespoons red wine vinegar

3 tablespoons quick-cooking tapioca

2 teaspoons minced garlic

½ teaspoon garlic salt

½ teaspoon ground black pepper

¼ teaspoon Tabasco®

2 (1-pound) packages "lite" kielbasa
 links, cut into ½-inch chunks
 (such as Hillshire Farms®)

1. Stir together all ingredients except the kielbasa in the slow cooker crock. Add the kielbasa and stir to coat with sauce.

2. Cover and cook 4 hours on LOW, stirring several times during cooking. To serve, switch the slow cooker to WARM setting.

Barbecue Kielbasa

Serves 12 (about ½ cup each)

These savory sausage bites are a favorite for fall and winter get-togethers. Luckily, they're also very cook-friendly—easy to make and easily served directly from the slow cooker. Keep plenty of toothpicks and napkins close by.

1. Stir together all ingredients except the kielbasa in the slow cooker crock. Then add the kielbasa and stir to coat with sauce.

2. Cover and cook 4 hours on LOW, stirring several times during cooking. To serve, switch the slow cooker to WARM setting.

INGREDIENT INFO If you prefer, regular kielbasa could be used instead of the "lite" variety that we like. We do not recommend using turkey kielbasa in this dish, as it tends to get tough during cooking.

1 (6-ounce) can tomato paste

⅔ cup water

2 tablespoons GF Barbecue Seasoning (page 201)

2 teaspoons white vinegar

½ teaspoon smoked paprika or liquid smoke (such as Colgin®)

2 (1-pound) packages "lite" kielbasa links, cut into ¾-inch chunks (such as Hillshire Farms®)

7

Soups, Stews, and Chili

Recipe Variation

DAIRY-FREE

Creamy Butternut Pear Soup

Serves 4 (about 1¾ cups each)

Warm, creamy, and packed with fall produce and spices, this wintry soup is perfect when you're craving something simple and wholesome. Reheated leftover soup and gluten-free crackers (such as Mary's Gone Crackers®) make a tasty lunch.

1 tablespoon butter

2 large carrots, peeled and chopped

1¼ pounds butternut squash, peeled and cut into 1–inch chunks

1 medium onion, finely chopped

2 ripe pears, any variety, cored and chopped (no need to peel)

3 cups vegetable broth (such as Pacific Natural Foods®)

1 teaspoon kosher salt

½ teaspoon ground nutmeg

¼ teaspoon garlic salt

¼ teaspoon ground black pepper

⅛ teaspoon ground ginger

⅛ teaspoon ground cinnamon

½ cup half-and-half

2 tablespoons snipped, fresh chives (optional)

1. Coat the inside of the slow cooker crock with the butter (leave excess in the crock). Add the carrots and squash to the crock. Sprinkle the onions and pears on top.

2. Whisk together the broth and the spices. Pour the mixture over the vegetables and pears in the crock (do not stir).

3. Cover and cook 8–10 hours on LOW (or 4–5 hours on HIGH).

4. Add the half-and-half to the crock and stir to combine. Puree the soup with an immersion blender until smooth. Alternatively, you can puree the soup in a food processor or blender (but be careful because the soup will be very hot).

5. To serve, divide between bowls and garnish each portion with a sprinkling of chives, if desired.

Dairy-Free Variation

Replace butter with canola oil.
Use soy milk in place of half-and-half.

Restaurant-Style "Baked" Potato Soup

Serves 6 (about 1½ cups each)

This rich, creamy soup is very popular in restaurants, so why not create a version at home that is supereasy to make and safe to eat? This is a fun dinner for a relaxed Friday night at home. Set up a topping bar in the middle of the table, and serve the soup with a big green salad.

1. Stir together all the ingredients except the milk and sour cream in the slow cooker crock.

2. Cover and cook 8–10 hours on LOW (or 4–5 hours on HIGH).

3. Stir in the milk and sour cream. Puree the soup with an immersion blender until desired consistency. (It could be chunky or smooth, depending on your preference.) Alternatively, you can puree the soup in a food processor or blender (but be careful because the soup will be very hot).

4. Offer desired toppings on the side so people can garnish their soup individually.

2 celery stalks, finely chopped

2 carrots, peeled and finely chopped

2 pounds russet potatoes, peeled and cut into 1-inch chunks

1 medium onion, finely chopped

1 (32-ounce) package chicken broth (such as Pacific Natural Foods®)

1 tablespoon quick-cooking tapioca

1 teaspoon minced garlic

1 teaspoon kosher salt

¼ teaspoon ground black pepper

1 cup milk

½ cup sour cream

Topping Ingredients

¾ cup real bacon bits (such as Hormel®)

1½ cups shredded cheddar cheese

1 bunch scallions or chives, thinly sliced

hot sauce (such as Frank's®)

Seafood Chowder

Serves 6 (about 1½ cups each)

Dairy ingredients cannot be slow cooked without curdling, so milk-based chowders can be a challenge. What's more, traditional chowders are thickened with flour— potentially double trouble. What we have learned over years of slow cooking is that tapioca makes a good thickener for chowder and is easy to use. As for the dairy component, simply add the milk, cream, or whatever the recipe calls for (our chowder uses both) at the end of the cooking time and heat through. It's so easy!

3 celery stalks, finely chopped

2 (6.5-ounce) cans chopped clams

1½ pounds of round, white potatoes, peeled and cut into 1-inch chunks

1 onion, finely chopped

1 (8-ounce) bottle clam juice

¼ cup water

¼ cup dry white wine

2 tablespoons quick-cooking tapioca

1 tablespoon butter

½ teaspoon kosher salt

¼ teaspoon ground black pepper

¼ teaspoon dried thyme

¼ teaspoon Tabasco® or more to taste

1 bay leaf

Finishing ingredients

1 cup light cream

½ cup milk

1 pound large shrimp (41–50) peeled, deveined, and tails removed

½ pound bay scallops

¼ cup finely chopped fresh parsley or thinly sliced chives (optional)

1. Stir together all chowder base ingredients in the slow cooker crock. Cook for 8 hours on LOW (or 4 hours on HIGH).

2. Stir in the cream, milk, shrimp, and scallops. Cover and heat on HIGH for 20–30 minutes until the chowder is heated through and the seafood is cooked.

3. Before serving, garnish each bowl with parsley, if desired.

New England Fish Chowder Variation

IN STEP 1: Omit the canned clams and add a second bottle of **clam juice**.

IN STEP 2: Omit the shrimp and scallops. Instead, use 1½ pounds **chowder fish** (such as a mix of haddock, cod, hake, and pollack), cut into 2-inch chunks.

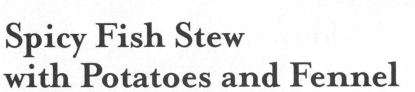

Spicy Fish Stew with Potatoes and Fennel

Serves 6 (about 1¾ cups each)

Kimberly loves the classic Italian sauté of fresh fennel, garlic, and crushed red pepper and thought it might translate nicely into a soup. With the addition of bright tomatoes, hearty potatoes, and flaky fish, we think this is a winner.

1. Stir together the stew base ingredients in the slow cooker crock. Cover and cook 8 hours on LOW (or 4 hours on HIGH).

2. Stir in the finishing ingredients (fish and lemon juice). Cover and heat on HIGH for 15–20 minutes until the chowder is heated through and the fish is cooked.

3. Stir gently before serving so that the fish stays in large pieces.

INGREDIENT INFO Fresh fennel is an underappreciated member of the vegetable family. Served raw, it is supercrisp with just a hint of licorice flavor. When cooked, especially in stews, it adds a pleasant layer of flavor and texture without adding lots of calories. This is a great starter recipe for the fennel-shy.

2 small heads of fennel (about 1½ pounds), ends trimmed and finely chopped

1½ pounds round, white potatoes, peeled and cut into 1-inch chunks

1 (35-ounce) can whole tomatoes, coarsely chopped, not drained

1 leek, washed well, halved lengthwise, and finely chopped

1 shallot, finely chopped

1 (8-ounce) bottle clam juice

⅓ cup dry white wine

2 tablespoons olive oil

1 bay leaf

2 teaspoons minced garlic ·

1 teaspoon oregano

¾ teaspoon kosher salt

½ teaspoon crushed red pepper or more to taste

¼ teaspoon ground black pepper

Finishing ingredients

1½ pounds mild white fish (haddock, cod, pollack, or hake), cut into 2-inch chunks

2 tablespoons fresh lemon juice

Lemony Chicken Soup with Kale and Potatoes

Serves 8 (about 1½ cups each)

This hearty chicken soup is perfect for those fall days when the air starts to take on a chill. Leftovers reheat nicely, and the soup freezes well, so it's an ideal make-ahead meal for a busy week.

3 round, white potatoes, peeled and cut into 1-inch chunks

2 carrots, finely chopped

2 celery stalks, finely chopped

1 onion, finely chopped

2 teaspoons minced garlic

2 tablespoons butter

½ teaspoon ground black pepper

1 teaspoon Tabasco®

1 ½ teaspoons dried oregano

4 cups thinly sliced chopped kale (discard thick stems before chopping)

2 pounds boneless, skinless chicken thighs, trimmed of excess fat and cut into bite-sized pieces

7 cups chicken broth (such as Pacific Natural Foods®)

1 lemon, washed and halved

1. Layer all ingredients in the slow cooker crock, starting with the potatoes on the bottom and ending with the lemon. Do not stir.

2. Cover and cook 8–10 hours on LOW (or 4–5 hours on HIGH). Using tongs, transfer the lemon halves to a small bowl. Using a fork, gently press the juice out of the lemons and add the juice back to the crock (discard the rinds).

3. Stir well and serve.

Dairy-Free Variation

Replace butter with olive oil.

NUTRITION NOTE Sometimes using unfamiliar greens can be intimidating, but kale deserves to be on your plate (or bowl, in this case). It's an excellent source of antioxidant vitamins A and C, as well as vitamin K. Kale is also a good source of fiber. Using greens in soups is an easy way to start working more of them into your diet.

Chicken Sausage and Vegetable Stew

Serves 8 (about 1¾ cups each)

This is such a pretty (and healthy) stew. Cut the potatoes, carrots, zucchini, and sausage roughly the same size for the most attractive presentation. No worries if you don't have a crowd to feed— leftover soup makes a wonderful brown-bag lunch.

1. Sprinkle the tapioca into the slow cooker crock. Add the bouillon, olive oil, garlic, oregano, bay leaf, kosher salt, and red pepper to the crock. Layer the vegetables, sausage, tomatoes, and water into the crock, starting with the potatoes and ending with the water. Do not stir.

2. Cover and cook 8 hours on LOW (or 4 hours on HIGH).

3. Before serving, stir the parsley into the soup. Garnish each bowl with some freshly ground pepper and a small drizzle of extra-virgin olive oil, if desired.

Dairy-Free Variation

Use dairy-free sausage.

2 tablespoons quick-cooking tapioca

2 teaspoons chicken or vegetable bouillon (such as Organic Better than Bouillon®)

1 tablespoon olive oil

1 teaspoon minced garlic

1 teaspoon oregano

1 bay leaf

¾ teaspoon kosher salt, more to taste

⅛ teaspoon crushed red pepper, more to taste

1 pound round, white potatoes, chopped

2 carrots, peeled, quartered lengthwise, and chopped

2 celery stalks, halved lengthwise and chopped

1 medium onion, finely chopped

2 medium zucchini, chopped

1 (9-ounce) package frozen cut green beans, thawed

1 (12-ounce) package precooked Italian chicken sausage (such as Al Fresco®), quartered lengthwise and chopped

2 (14.5-ounce) cans diced tomatoes

3½ cups water

⅓ cup finely chopped fresh parsley

freshly ground black pepper (optional)

extra-virgin olive oil (optional)

Chili Verde with Turkey

Serves 6 (about 1½ cups each)

2 tablespoons olive oil

1 pound lean ground turkey

1 sweet onion, finely chopped

1 tablespoon minced garlic

2 (4-ounce) cans green chilies

1 ½ cups chicken broth
   (such as Pacific Natural Foods®)

3 Italian frying peppers

2 pounds tomatillos,
   husked and chopped

1 green bell pepper, finely chopped

1 jalapeño, seeded and finely minced,
   or more to taste

1 tablespoon honey

1 tablespoon quick-cooking tapioca

1 tablespoon chicken bouillon (such as
   Organic Better than Bouillon®)

1 tablespoon Tabasco® Green Jalapeño
   Pepper Sauce Jalapeño

1 tablespoon cumin

1½ teaspoons dried oregano

1 teaspoon kosher salt or more to taste

½ teaspoon ground chipotle

¼ teaspoon ground black pepper

⅓ cup finely chopped cilantro

lime (optional)

avocado (optional)

Chili Verde is a Mexican stew made with tomatillos, peppers, and braised pork shoulder. To make our version a little lighter, we replaced the pork with ground turkey. None of the store-bought green enchilada sauces we found were "safe," so we went the homemade route. If you have difficulty locating Italian frying peppers, substitute Anaheim peppers or yellow bell peppers. Don't be put off by the rather lengthy ingredient list—it all comes together easily.

1. Heat the oil in a large skillet over medium heat. When hot, add the turkey, onion, and garlic. Cook and stir until the onion is soft and the meat is browned, about 10 minutes.

2. While the turkey cooks, add remaining ingredients (except for the cilantro, limes, and avocados) to the slow cooker crock and stir well.

3. Stir the cooked turkey mixture into the chili mixture. Cover and cook 8–10 hours on LOW (or 4–5 hours on HIGH).

4. Before serving, stir in the fresh cilantro. Garnish bowls with lime wedges and chopped avocado, if desired.

INGREDIENT INFO Tomatillos are a member of the gooseberry family, though they're often confused with green tomatoes. Their papery husks are generally easy to remove; a little warm water will loosen any sticky husks.

Yellow Split Pea Soup with Crispy Prosciutto

Serves 8 (about 1½ cups each)

Our hearty version of split pea soup was born of a coffee-fueled collaboration. We can't tell you how thrilled we were to discover that prosciutto di Parma is gluten-free! A bit of this celebrated Italian ham is used to season the soup, while the rest is crisped up in a frying pan for a restaurant-quality garnish.

1. Cut the prosciutto into thin strips and add half of it to the slow cooker crock. Refrigerate the other half.

2. Stir together remaining ingredients in the slow cooker crock. Cover and cook 8 hours on LOW (or 4 hours on HIGH).

3. Shortly before serving the soup, prepare the garnish. Add the reserved strips of prosciutto to a medium, nonstick skillet over medium heat. Cook and stir until crispy, 8–10 minutes. Use a slotted spoon to transfer prosciutto to a plate lined with paper towels.

4. Stir soup well before serving. Garnish each bowl with 2 tablespoons of the crispy prosciutto.

Dairy-Free Variation

Replace butter with olive oil.

½ pound thinly sliced prosciutto di Parma, divided

2 (32-ounce) packages chicken broth (such as Pacific Natural Foods®)

4 carrots, peeled, halved lengthwise, and thinly sliced

2 leeks, halved lengthwise and thinly sliced

2 celery stalks, finely chopped

2 shallots, finely chopped

1 pound round, white potatoes, peeled and cut into ½-inch pieces

2 cups yellow split peas, rinsed and picked over

2 tablespoons butter

½ teaspoon dried thyme

¼ teaspoon salt

¼ teaspoon ground black pepper

Pork Posole

Serves 8 (about 1⅓ cups each)

A classic pork and corn stew from Mexico, posole can be made spicy or mild to suit your taste. Our version has more tomatoes than traditional posole, adding a more vibrant flavor to the mixture. The garnishes make this meal fun for any little eaters in your household.

1. Stir together the stew ingredients in the slow cooker crock.

2. Cover and cook 8 hours on LOW (or 4 hours on HIGH). Stir before serving the posole in bowls with garnishes on the side.

Dairy-Free Variation

Omit sour cream garnish.

> **NUTRITION NOTE** Hominy is a type of hulled corn that has been stripped of its outer fibers (bran and germ). It is generally sold canned, alongside canned beans at the supermarket. If you cannot find it in your local market, substitute 1 pound frozen corn, thawed.

1½ pounds boneless pork sirloin, cut into 1-inch chunks

1 pound tomatillos, husked and chopped

1 medium onion, finely chopped

1 green or yellow bell pepper, finely chopped

2 (14.5-ounce) cans petite diced tomatoes

2 (15-ounce) cans white hominy, rinsed and drained

½ cup water

1 tablespoon minced garlic

1 tablespoon quick-cooking tapioca

1 tablespoon Tabasco® Jalapeño Green Pepper Sauce

1 tablespoon tomato paste

2 teaspoons chicken bouillon (such as Organic Better than Bouillon®)

2 teaspoons ground cumin

2 teaspoons dried oregano

1 teaspoon cider vinegar

1 teaspoon ground chipotle

½ teaspoon kosher salt

⅛ teaspoon crushed red pepper or more to taste (optional)

Garnishes

sour cream

finely chopped fresh cilantro or thinly sliced scallions

avocado, chopped

corn chips (such as Tostitos® Natural Blue Corn Restaurant-Style Tortilla Chips)

"Deconstructed" Stuffed Cabbage Stew

Serves 8 (about 1¼ cups each)

We adore stuffed cabbage, but when time is short, this is our go-to recipe. It's got everything we like about stuffed cabbage, without the fuss.

1. Warm the oil in a medium stock pot over medium heat. Add the beef and onion; cook until onion is soft and meat is browned throughout, about 8 minutes. Drain off the fat. Stir in the tomatoes, bouillon, sugar, Italian seasoning, garlic, pepper, and Tabasco; mix well and set aside.

2. Place the chopped cabbage in the slow cooker crock. Sprinkle the rice over the cabbage. Spread the beef mixture over the rice; do not stir. Pour the beef broth over all; do not stir.

3. Cover and cook 8 hours on LOW (4 hours on HIGH). Stir the soup well before serving. Garnish each portion with shredded Parmesan, if desired.

Dairy-Free Variation

Omit Parmesan garnish.

INGREDIENT INFO Adding a little sugar to a recipe in which tomatoes figure prominently, as we do here (spaghetti sauce is another example), tempers the acidity that the tomatoes contribute to the dish. It should not make the end product sweet (if it does, too much sugar has been added). If you'd prefer, leave it out.

1 tablespoon olive oil

1¼ pounds lean ground beef (at least 90 percent lean)

1 medium onion, chopped

1 (28-ounce) can diced tomatoes

1 tablespoon beef bouillon (such as Organic Better than Bouillon®)

1 tablespoon sugar (optional)

1½ teaspoons Italian seasoning

1 teaspoon minced garlic

½ teaspoon ground black pepper

¼ teaspoon Tabasco®

½ head cabbage (about 1½ pounds), chopped

¾ cup brown rice

1 (32-ounce) package beef broth (such as Pacific Natural Foods®)

shredded Parmesan cheese (optional)

Lamb Tagine

Serves 6 (about 1⅓ cups each)

A *tagine* is a Moroccan dish that is named after the ceramic, lidded pot that it's cooked in. This particular *tagine* uses dates to sweeten the spiced broth, and it is especially good with Cauliflower Couscous (see page 198) or over basmati rice.

2 pounds lamb stew meat, trimmed and cut into 1½-inch chunks

2 cups water

3 carrots, halved lengthwise and sliced on the diagonal

3 celery stalks, sliced on the diagonal

1 sweet onion, finely chopped

1 (19-ounce) can chickpeas, rinsed and drained

½ pound Medjool dates, pitted and quartered lengthwise

2 tablespoons fresh lemon juice

1 tablespoons honey

1 tablespoon grated fresh ginger or 1 teaspoon ground ginger

2 teaspoons chicken bouillon (such as Organic Better than Bouillon®)

1 teaspoon minced garlic

1 teaspoon kosher salt

1 teaspoon fresh lemon zest or orange zest

1 teaspoon ground turmeric

1 teaspoon paprika

1 teaspoon ground cumin

½ teaspoon ground cinnamon

½ teaspoon ground black pepper

⅛ teaspoon ground cayenne pepper

Garnishes

1 cup coarsely chopped pistachios

½ cup finely chopped mint

1. Stir together all *tagine* ingredients in the slow cooker crock. Cover and cook 8–10 hours on LOW (or 4–5 hours on HIGH).

2. Skim any visible fat that has come to the surface of the stew and discard. Stir well. Garnish each bowl with about 2½ tablespoons pistachios and a generous tablespoon of mint.

Beef and Bean Soup

Serves 8 (about 1¾ cups each)

This comforting soup is richly flavored with beans, tomatoes, and beef. Perfect for a busy workday, since it can withstand a long cook time, it's also budget-friendly. Stew meat is a useful item to have on hand; we like to stock up on stew meat when it's on special sale and freeze it for later use.

DAIRY-FREE

1. Stir together all ingredients in the slow cooker crock. Cover and cook 8–10 hours on LOW (or 4–5 hours on HIGH).

2. Remove the bay leaf, stir well, and serve.

NUTRITION NOTE If you're concerned about sodium in your diet, look for reduced-sodium broth and bouillon (always check the ingredients to make sure they are gluten-free as well as low in sodium), and get in the habit of rinsing canned beans. Research has shown that draining and rinsing canned beans can decrease their sodium content by 40 percent—definitely worth doing!

1 (32-ounce) package beef broth (such as Pacific Natural Foods®)

2 (15.5-ounce) cans cannellini beans, rinsed and drained

2 (14.5-ounce) cans diced tomatoes

1½ pounds beef stew meat, cut into 1-inch pieces

2 carrots, finely chopped

1 onion, finely chopped

1 bay leaf

2 tablespoons extra-virgin olive oil

2 tablespoons real bacon bits (such as Hormel®)

1 tablespoon red wine vinegar

2 teaspoons minced garlic

2 teaspoons beef bouillon (such as Organic Better than Bouillon®)

1 teaspoon dried oregano

½ teaspoon cumin

½ teaspoon celery seed

¼ teaspoon kosher salt or more to taste

¼ teaspoon ground black pepper

pinch crushed red pepper or more to taste

Smoky and Spicy Beef Taco Soup

Serves 6 (about 1⅓ cups each)

1½ pounds lean stew beef, cut into
  1-inch pieces

2 (14.5-ounce) cans diced tomatoes

1 (15.5-ounce) can pinto beans,
  drained and rinsed

1 (4-ounce) can diced green chilies

2 cups water

1 jalapeño, seeded and minced

2 tablespoons dried minced onion

1 tablespoon tomato paste

2 teaspoons beef bouillon (such as
  Organic Better than Bouillon®)

1½ teaspoons cumin

1 teaspoon Tabasco® or more to taste

1 teaspoon ground chipotle

1 teaspoon smoked paprika

1 teaspoon oregano

1 teaspoon minced garlic

¼ teaspoon kosher salt

¼ teaspoon ground black pepper

Garnishes

2 avocados, diced

1½ cups grated cheddar cheese

corn chips (such as Tostitos®)

A spicy tomato broth seasoned with smoky chipotle peppers forms the base of this hearty beef-and-bean-packed soup. Perfect for weeknight cooking, this soup can easily withstand a longer cooking time, if needed, to accommodate a long workday.

1. Stir together all the soup ingredients in the slow cooker crock. Cover and cook 8–10 hours on LOW (or 4–5 hours on HIGH).

2. Stir well and divide between bowls. Offer garnishes family-style, so that diners can individualize their bowls.

Dairy-Free Variation

Omit cheddar cheese garnish.

Classic Beef and Vegetable Stew

Serves 6 (about 1½ cups each)

Full of potatoes, carrots, and chunks of beef simmered in a rich broth, this is the stew for you if you're craving your grandmother's cooking. One ingredient that adds to the stew's flavor is Bragg Liquid Aminos®, which is similar to soy sauce but safely gluten-free.

1. Stir together all ingredients in the slow cooker crock. Cover and cook 8–10 hours on LOW (or 4–5 hours on HIGH).

2. Stir well and remove bay leaf before serving.

INGREDIENT INFO Bragg Liquid Aminos® is a gluten-free, liquid protein concentrate that's derived from soybeans. It contains sixteen different amino acids and no added salt. We like to use it as a substitute for soy sauce, tamari, or Worcestershire. Locating Bragg Liquid Aminos® in your store may not be easy. Most natural food and health food stores carry it, often on the shelf with vinegars or soy sauce. In a regular supermarket, check the "healthy food aisle" or the Asian foods section.

2½ cups water

2 pounds round, white potatoes, peeled and cut into 1-inch cubes

1½ pounds stew beef

3 large carrots, peeled and cut into ¼-inch slices

2 celery stalks, finely chopped

1 medium onion, finely chopped

1 (8-ounce) package sliced baby bella mushrooms

2 tablespoons tomato paste

2 tablespoons quick-cooking tapioca

1 tablespoon olive oil

1 tablespoon Bragg Liquid Aminos®

2 teaspoons beef bouillon (such as Organic Better than Bouillon®)

2 teaspoons minced garlic

¾ teaspoon dried thyme

½ teaspoon kosher salt or more to taste

½ teaspoon ground black pepper

¼ teaspoon dried rosemary

1 bay leaf

Argentinean Vegetable and Beef Stew (Carbonada)

Serves 10 (about 1⅓ cups each)

2 (14.5-ounce) cans diced tomatoes

1 pound lean beef stew meat,
    cut into 1-inch chunks

1 green or red bell pepper, chopped

1 medium onion, finely chopped

¾ cup dry white wine

2 tablespoons olive oil

2 round, white potatoes,
    peeled and cut into 1-inch chunks

2 sweet potatoes,
    peeled and cut into 1-inch chunks

2 small zucchini or summer squash,
    chopped

2 pears, peeled and cut into
    1-inch chunks

½ pound frozen corn, thawed

1 cup water

¼ cup finely chopped dried apricots

2 teaspoons vegetable bouillon (such as
    Organic Better than Bouillon®)

2 teaspoons cider vinegar

1½ teaspoons oregano

1½ teaspoons minced garlic

1 bay leaf

½ teaspoon kosher salt or more to taste

½ teaspoon ground black pepper

Savory and sweet, Carbonada is a classic Argentinean dish—a very hearty vegetable stew with just a little meat for flavor. Kimberly had her doubts as she filled the slow cooker with white potatoes, sweet potatoes, yellow squash, and pears, but was quite delighted with the aromatic, tangy results. Serve our recipe for cornbread (see page 188) on the side for an authentic Argentinean meal.

1. Add all the ingredients to the slow cooker crock and stir well.

2. Cover and cook 10 hours on LOW (or 5 hours on HIGH).

3. Stir well before serving.

INGREDIENT INFO   In our Carbonada, dried apricots have been substituted for peaches, the traditional ingredient, because fresh peaches are not available year-round and canned peaches don't hold up during the long cooking time. Be sure to read the label on the packaging for dried apricots, since some dried fruit is processed in facilities where it can come into contact with wheat products. You'll probably have better luck with organic dried apricots. But be prepared—they won't look as pretty as fruit that has been treated with preservatives.

Monday Night Football Chili

Serves 6 (about 1½ cups each)

Monday Night Football Chili is game day fare at its best—lots of savory meat with just enough beans and tomatoes to call it chili. The ground meats need to be browned before slow cooking, but that's the only outside-the-crock cooking required.

1. In a large skillet over medium heat, cook the ground meats until no pink is showing, about 8 minutes. Drain meat and discard fat.

2. While the meats cook, add the remaining chili ingredients to the slow cooker. Add the cooked meats and stir well to combine. Cover and cook 8 hours on LOW (or 4 hours on HIGH).

3. Stir chili well before serving. Offer garnishes family-style.

Dairy-Free Variation

Omit cheese and sour cream garnishes.

---

1 pound lean ground beef

1 pound lean ground pork

1 tablespoon minced garlic

2 tablespoons GF Chili Powder (page 200)

1 onion, finely chopped

1 green pepper, finely chopped

2 (15.5-ounce) cans kidney beans or black beans

2 (14.5-ounce) cans diced tomatoes

2 tablespoons tomato paste

2 teaspoons beef bouillon (such as Organic Better than Bouillon®)

Garnishes

hot sauce

shredded cheddar cheese

thinly sliced scallions

sour cream

Cincinnati Chili ("Four-Way")

Serves 6 (about ¾ cup each)

If you've never had Cincinnati Chili, you're likely to be surprised not only by its complex taste, but by the way it's presented, too. With its roots in Greek cuisine, it offers a mix of sweet and hot spices—along with a tiny bit of cocoa (for an effect similar to that in Mexican mole). Cincinnati Chili is not supposed to set your mouth on fire like a Texas chili might. Rather, it's meant to be a subtle mélange of flavors—and for some it's an acquired taste.

1 pound ground chuck
1 large onion, chopped, divided
1 teaspoon minced garlic
½ teaspoon kosher salt
¼ teaspoon ground black pepper
1 (15-ounce) can tomato sauce
¾ cup water
1 tablespoon Bragg Liquid Aminos®
2 teaspoons cider vinegar
1 teaspoon unsweetened cocoa powder
1 teaspoon GF Chili Powder (page 200)
½ teaspoon cumin
½ teaspoon ground allspice
½ teaspoon cinnamon
¼ teaspoon ground ancho chili pepper
dash ground cloves
1½ cups grated cheddar cheese
10 ounces cooked spaghetti
   (such as Ancient Harvest®
   Quinoa Spaghetti)

The fun part is the way it's served. Traditionally, Cincinnati Chili is served on a plate: spaghetti topped with chili is a "Two-Way"; a "Three-Way" is served with grated cheddar cheese on top; and a "Four-Way" includes yet another ingredient on top—chopped onions. "Five-Way" is all of that, but with kidney beans heated separately and served either on top of the spaghetti or directly under it. One other thing: Cincinnati Chili is a great slow cooker recipe because the flavors blend nicely during the long cooking time. Feel free to let the chili sit overnight in the refrigerator to give the flavors more time to meld—but usually we can't hold off that long!

1. In a large skillet over medium heat, cook the ground chuck, half the chopped onion (reserve the remaining onion for topping the chili), garlic, salt, and pepper until the beef is cooked through and no more pink is showing, about 8 minutes.

2. While the meat cooks, add the remaining chili ingredients (except for the cheddar cheese, spaghetti, and reserved onion) to the slow cooker. Add the cooked meat mixture to the crock and stir well to combine. Cover and cook 6–8 hours on LOW (or 3–4 hours on HIGH).

3. Stir chili well before serving. To serve, divide the cooked spaghetti between six individual plates. Top with an equal portion of the chili, then ¼ cup of the cheddar cheese and a sprinkling of the reserved onion.

"Five-Way" Variation

IN STEP 3: Before plating the chili, heat a 15-ounce can of dark **red kidney beans** (rinse and drain them first, if you like) in the microwave on medium power for 2 minutes, or until hot. Spoon the hot beans onto the plates before adding the spaghetti, chili, and cheese. Or, if you prefer, spoon the hot beans on top of the chili, then top with the cheese and onion as directed.

Dairy-Free Variation

Omit cheddar cheese garnish.

8

Vegetarian

Tomato Basil Soup

Serves 6 (about 1½ cups each)

The addition of sun-dried tomatoes gives this soup a rich, tomato flavor. If you've been missing the classic grilled cheese sandwich and tomato soup lunch, pick up a loaf of Udi's gluten-free bread and go for it! This soup freezes well, and you can also use the finished soup as a base for several other soups (see variations on the following page).

1 (32-ounce) package vegetarian broth (such as Pacific Natural Foods®)

1 (28-ounce) can crushed tomatoes

2 cups water

⅓ cup sun-dried tomatoes

1 sweet onion, finely chopped

2 tablespoons butter or olive oil

1½ teaspoons minced garlic

1 teaspoon kosher salt

1 teaspoon red wine vinegar

1 teaspoon sugar

¼ teaspoon ground black pepper

pinch crushed red pepper

⅓ cup fresh basil leaves, thinly sliced

Optional garnishes

chopped olives

crumbled feta, chèvre, or grated Parmesan cheese

crumbled bacon

extra-virgin olive oil for drizzling

1. Stir together all soup ingredients except the fresh basil in the slow cooker crock. Cover and cook 8 hours on LOW (or 4 hours on HIGH).

2. Puree the soup with an immersion blender until smooth. Alternatively, you can puree the soup in a food processor or blender (but be careful because the soup will be very hot).

3. Stir in the fresh basil. Offer preferred garnishes on the side, if desired.

Dairy-Free Variation

Substitute olive oil for the butter.
Omit cheese garnish.

Vegetable and Bean Soup

IN STEP 3: In addition to the basil, stir in
1 teaspoon **oregano**, 1 (14-ounce) can **red
beans**, rinsed and drained, and 1 pound bag
frozen mixed vegetables, heated according
to package instructions. Stir well. Cover and
heat through for 20–30 minutes.

Creamy Tomato and Rice
(not dairy-free)

IN STEP 3: In addition to the basil, stir in
1½ cups cooked **rice** and ¼ cup **heavy
cream**. Stir well. Cover and heat through
for 20–30 minutes.

Hearty Spinach Minestrone

IN STEP 3: In addition to the basil, stir in
2 (14-ounce) cans **white beans**, rinsed and
drained; 2 (10-ounce) packages of frozen
chopped **spinach**, thawed and squeezed dry;
and 2 cups cooked and rinsed, gluten-free,
bite-size **pasta**. Stir well. Cover and heat
through for 20–30 minutes.

Indian-Spiced Carrot Ginger Soup

Serves 6 (about 1½ cups each)

A must-have in any soup lover's repertoire, this vegetarian carrot-ginger soup blends spicy and sweet tastes with creamy texture in every bite. Preparing this soup in the slow cooker allows all the flavors to marry, more so than they would if prepared on the stove-top.

1 (32-ounce) package vegetable broth (such as Pacific Natural Foods®)

1 large sweet onion, finely chopped

2 pounds carrots, peeled and finely chopped

2 tablespoons butter

2 tablespoons grated fresh ginger

2 tablespoons honey

1 tablespoon curry powder

1 teaspoon kosher salt or more to taste

1 teaspoon turmeric

1 teaspoon ground cumin

½ teaspoon paprika (smoked or sweet)

¼ teaspoon ground coriander

½ teaspoon Tabasco® or more to taste

1 (14-ounce) can coconut milk (regular or light)

finely chopped cilantro or thinly sliced chives (optional)

1. Stir together all ingredients except the cilantro in the slow cooker crock.

2. Cover and cook 8–10 hours on LOW (or 4–5 hours on HIGH).

3. Puree the soup with an immersion blender until smooth. Alternatively, you can puree the soup in a food processor or blender (but be careful because the soup will be very hot).

4. Garnish each bowl with a sprinkling of cilantro, if desired.

Dairy-Free Variation

Replace butter with coconut oil or olive oil.

TECHNIQUE TIP If you do not own an immersion blender, this recipe and our recipe for Root Vegetable Winter Warmer Soup (page 89) might convince you to purchase one. It's a handy piece of equipment to have in the kitchen for making pureed soups, homemade salad dressings, and all kinds of smoothies.

Greek Chickpea Soup *(Revithia)*

DAIRY-FREE

Serves 6 (about 1⅓ cups each)

Kimberly discovered *revithia* in the pages of Hannaford supermarket's *FRESH* magazine and it soon became a favorite in her kitchen. The original recipe called for canned chickpeas, but when using a slow cooker, use dried chickpeas instead (because of the longer cooking time). This soup is very budget-friendly and freezes well for future meals. Serve it with a yummy Greek salad for a complete meal.

1. Stir together all the ingredients except lemon juice and parsley in the slow cooker crock. Cover and cook 10 hours on LOW (or 5 hours on HIGH).

2. Before serving, test the tenderness of the chickpeas. If they are tender, stir in the lemon juice. Use an immersion blender to process half of the soup into a puree. Alternatively, you can puree the soup in a food processor or blender (but be careful because the soup will be very hot). The soup should be smooth with some whole chickpeas and bits of onions.

3. Garnish each bowl with a good drizzle of olive oil and a bit of parsley, if desired.

1 pound dry chickpeas, picked over and soaked overnight or quick-soaked (see page 25 for soaking instructions)

5 cups water

3 tablespoons finely chopped fresh rosemary or fresh sage

1 large sweet onion, finely chopped

2 tablespoons extra-virgin olive oil, plus more for garnishing

2 teaspoons minced garlic

2 teaspoons kosher salt

½ teaspoon ground black pepper

pinch of crushed red pepper

3 tablespoons lemon juice

finely chopped parsley (optional)

Curried Cauliflower and White Bean Soup

Serves 4 (about 2 cups each)

This satisfying soup is packed with healthful ingredients—cauliflower, sweet potatoes, beans—and Indian flavors. The ingredients require a little prep time, but the soup itself doesn't get any easier than this.

1 (16-ounce) bag frozen cauliflower florets, thawed

1 leek, trimmed, washed well, and thinly sliced

1 tablespoon plus 1 teaspoon curry powder

¼ teaspoon cayenne pepper or more to taste

½ teaspoon ground cumin

1 teaspoon grated fresh ginger

½ teaspoon kosher salt or more to taste

1 (32-ounce) container vegetable broth (such as Pacific Natural Foods®)

1 pound sweet potatoes, peeled and cut into 1-inch chunks

2 (15.5-ounce) cans cannellini beans, rinsed and drained

¼ cup plain crème fraiche, Greek yogurt, or sour cream (optional)

2 tablespoons finely chopped fresh cilantro (optional)

1. Stir together all ingredients except the crème fraiche and cilantro in the slow cooker crock. Cover and cook 8 hours on LOW (or 4 hours on HIGH).

2. Stir well before serving. Garnish bowls with crème fraiche and cilantro, if desired.

Dairy-Free Variation

Omit crème fraiche garnish.

TECHNIQUE TIP It's a good idea to thaw frozen ingredients *before* adding them to the slow cooker crock. Extreme temperature changes as the slow cooker starts to heat the frozen food can cause the crock to crack.

Root Vegetable Winter Warmer Soup

Serves 8 (about 1½ cups each)

As the temperature dips, nothing warms an evening like homemade soup. A superb mix of carrots, parsnips, potatoes, and sweet potatoes is the backbone of this nourishing recipe.

1. Stir together all ingredients except the crème fraiche and chives in the slow cooker crock. Cover and cook 8–10 hours on LOW (or 4–5 hours on HIGH).

2. Puree the soup with an immersion blender until smooth. Alternatively, you can puree the soup in a food processor or blender (but be careful because the soup will be very hot).

3. Stir well. Garnish each bowl with a touch of crème fraiche and a sprinkle of chives, if desired.

Dairy-Free Variation

Replace butter with olive oil.
Omit crème fraiche garnish.

INGREDIENT INFO   Although it's rather pricey in the supermarket (when you can find it), crème fraiche is easy and inexpensive to make at home. Combine ¼ cup sour cream with ¾ cup heavy cream in a jar, and shake well to combine. Leave at room temperature for 12-24 hours, until the mixture thickens. (It will take less time in summer than in winter.) Refrigerate crème fraiche until needed. Use leftover crème fraiche as a topping for fresh fruit or spooned over chocolate ice cream. (This may sound strange, but give it a go—it's very tasty!)

2 (32-ounce) packages vegetable broth (such as Pacific Natural Foods®)

6 carrots, peeled and sliced

1 sweet potato (about 1 pound), peeled and chopped

2 russet potatoes (about 1½ pounds), peeled and chopped

2 celery stalks, chopped

3 parsnips, peeled and sliced

1 medium Vidalia onion, chopped

2 tablespoons butter or olive oil

2 tablespoons honey

2 tablespoons Bragg Liquid Aminos®

1 tablespoon lemon juice

½ teaspoon thyme

¼ teaspoon Tabasco® or more to taste

½ teaspoon kosher salt or more to taste

crème fraiche (optional)

thinly sliced fresh chives (optional)

2 carrots, finely chopped

1¼ cups French green lentils
(also called lentilles du Puy),
rinsed and picked over

2 celery stalks, finely chopped

3 shallots, finely chopped

1 leek, trimmed, washed well,
and thinly sliced

1 teaspoon minced garlic

1 tablespoon olive oil

½ teaspoon kosher salt
or more to taste

¼ teaspoon ground black pepper
or more to taste

1 bay leaf

¾ teaspoon dried thyme

2 (14.5-ounce) cans diced tomatoes

6 cups vegetable broth
(such as Pacific Natural Foods®)

Pistou ingredients

2 cups fresh basil leaves
or fresh parsley leaves,
or a combination of the two

¼ teaspoon kosher salt

pinch ground black pepper

zest and juice of 1 lemon

2 cloves garlic

3 tablespoons extra-virgin olive oil

¼ cup grated Parmesan cheese

⅓ cup grated Parmesan
or crumbled feta cheese
(optional garnish)

French Lentil Soup with Lemony Pistou

Serves 6 (about 2 cups each)

Some people prefer French green lentils to other lentil varieties because they hold their shape so well during cooking and have a rich, appealing color. However, don't fret if you can't find French lentils; simply substitute regular lentils. In either case, don't skip the pistou. It's an embellishment that really makes this soup special and is definitely worth the extra step.

1. Layer all the soup ingredients in the crock, starting with the carrots on the bottom and ending with the broth. Do not stir. Cover and cook 8–10 hours on LOW (or 4–5 hours on HIGH).

2. To make the pistou, add all the ingredients except cheese to a food processor and process until smooth. Transfer mixture to a bowl and stir in ¼ cup grated Parmesan. Refrigerate pistou until needed, but bring it to room temperature before serving.

3. Stir soup well and divide between bowls. Garnish each bowl with a generous tablespoon of pistou and a sprinkling of Parmesan or feta cheese, if desired.

Dairy-Free Variation

Omit Parmesan cheese.

Brazilian Black Bean Soup

Serves 8 (about 1½ cups each)

We love the delicate orange accent in this easy, economical black bean soup. Serve it over steamed rice if that suits your taste, or alongside some homemade cornbread (page 188). This soup freezes and reheats well.

1. Stir together the first 16 ingredients (black beans through black pepper) in the slow cooker crock. Cover and cook 8–10 hours on LOW (or 4–5 hours on HIGH). The beans should be tender.

2. Stir in the orange juice. Use an immersion blender to puree some of the soup. This will thicken the soup while still leaving some whole beans intact. Alternatively, you can puree the soup in a food processor or blender (but be careful because the soup will be very hot).

3. Cover and cook an additional 30 minutes. Garnish each bowl with cilantro and sour cream, if desired.

Dairy-Free Variation

Omit sour cream garnish.

1 pound dry black beans, picked over, and soaked overnight or quick-soaked (see page 25 for soaking instructions)

1 (32-ounce) package vegetarian broth (such as Pacific Natural Foods®)

1 sweet onion, chopped

1 red or green bell pepper, chopped

2 carrots, peeled and chopped

2 celery stalks, chopped

1 jalapeño, seeded and finely chopped

2 tablespoons olive oil

1 tablespoon minced garlic

1 tablespoon ground cumin

2 teaspoons oregano

1½ teaspoon kosher salt or more to taste

½ teaspoon smoked paprika

1 teaspoon orange zest

1 teaspoon Tabasco® or more to taste

½ teaspoon ground black pepper

1 cup orange juice

¼ cup finely chopped cilantro or parsley (optional)

sour cream (optional)

Butter Bean Stew with Sweet Potatoes and Wild Rice

Serves 8 (about 1½ cups each)

¾ cup wild rice

2 carrots, peeled, halved lengthwise, and cut into ½-inch slices

2 parsnips, peeled, halved lengthwise, and cut into ½-inch slices

3 celery stalks, cut into ½-inch slices

2 leeks, washed well, halved lengthwise, and thinly sliced

2 sweet potatoes (about 2 pounds), peeled and chopped into bite-sized pieces

2 teaspoons minced garlic

1½ teaspoons kosher salt or more to taste

½ teaspoon ground black pepper

¼ teaspoon crushed red pepper

1 (32-ounce) package vegetable broth (such as Pacific Natural Foods®)

3 cups water

2 tablespoons extra-virgin olive oil

1 tablespoon Bragg Liquid Aminos®

2 (15-ounce) cans butter beans

¼ cup finely chopped fresh dill

2 tablespoons fresh lemon juice

2 tablespoons finely chopped fresh parsley

1 tablespoon finely chopped fresh rosemary

This hearty vegetable stew is brightened at the end of cooking with the addition of fresh herbs and lemon juice. Chopping the carrots, parsnips, and celery so they are roughly the size of a butter bean will enhance the overall appearance of the soup and help everything cook evenly. You will need at least a six-quart slow cooker to handle this amount of stew, but if you have a smaller machine, just halve the ingredients. This stew will hold well in the refrigerator for several days, or you can freeze some for later (it reheats really well).

1. Layer the first 15 ingredients (wild rice through butter beans) into the slow cooker crock as listed; do not stir.

2. Cover and cook 10 hours on LOW (or 5 hours on HIGH). The wild rice should be cooked through and tender.

3. Stir in the fresh herbs and lemon juice and serve.

Corn Chowder

Serves 8 (about 1¼ cups each)

Many corn chowder recipes rely on creamed corn to thicken the broth. Unfortunately for gluten-free folks, many companies will not specify how much modified food starch is contained in creamed corn, so we've taken the safe route and thickened this chowder with cornmeal and cornstarch. Smoked paprika adds a nice depth to the flavor of this chowder. For a complete meal, serve this with a salad and Scallion and Cheddar Cornbread (page 189).

1. Stir together the canned corn, cornstarch, and cornmeal in a medium mixing bowl. Use an immersion blender to puree the mixture. (Alternatively, you could process the ingredients in a blender or food processor.) Transfer the mixture to the slow cooker crock.

2. Stir in the next 10 ingredients (potatoes through bay leaf), mixing well. Cover and cook 8 hours on LOW (or 4 hours on HIGH).

3. Stir in thawed corn, milk, half-and-half, and hot sauce. Cover and cook another 30 minutes on LOW (or 15 minutes on HIGH). Garnish each bowl with fresh parsley, if desired.

1 (14-ounce) can corn

2 tablespoons cornstarch

2 tablespoons cornmeal

1½ pounds round white potatoes, peeled and cut into bite-sized pieces

1 onion, chopped

2 stalks celery, finely chopped

2 cups vegetable broth (such as Pacific Natural Foods®)

2 tablespoons butter

1 teaspoon kosher salt

½ teaspoon ground black pepper

¼ teaspoon smoked paprika

¼ teaspoon dried thyme

1 bay leaf

1 pound frozen corn, thawed

1½ cups milk

⅓ cup half-and-half

½ teaspoon hot sauce (such as Frank's®)

finely chopped fresh parsley or chives (optional)

Quinoa and Bean Chili

Serves 6 (about 1½ cups each)

1 cup red quinoa

2 (15.5-ounce) cans red kidney beans

2 (14.5-ounce) can diced tomatoes

2½ cups water

1 medium onion, finely chopped

1 green or red bell pepper, finely chopped

1 jalapeño, seeded and minced,
*   or more to taste*

1 bay leaf

2 tablespoons finely chopped
*   sun-dried tomatoes*

2 tablespoons olive oil

1 tablespoon tomato paste

1 tablespoon vegetable bouillon (such as
*   Organic Better than Bouillon®)*

1 tablespoon lemon juice or lime juice

1 tablespoon honey

2 teaspoons ground cumin

2 teaspoons dried oregano

1 teaspoon garlic powder

1 teaspoon ground chipotle powder

1 teaspoon paprika (smoked or sweet)

½ teaspoon kosher salt

½ teaspoon ground black pepper

DAIRY-FREE

Red quinoa and red kidney beans provide the protein in this meat-free chili, and ground chipotle chilies, fresh jalapeños, and paprika provide the spice. Even meat lovers will be happy with this substantial chili. Serve it with corn chips or homemade cornbread (page 188). This recipe freezes and reheats well.

1. Stir together all ingredients in the slow cooker crock. Cover and cook 8–10 hours on LOW (or 4–5 hours on HIGH).

2. Remove bay leaf and stir well before serving.

Three-Bean Chili with Avocado Salsa

Serves 10 (about 1 cup each)

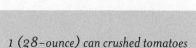

This classic vegetarian chili is accented with smoky, sweet, roasted red peppers and topped with a vibrant avocado lime salsa. Cook this on a workday—it'll be just fine if you're late getting home.

1. Stir together all chili ingredients in the slow cooker crock. Cover and cook 8–10 hours on LOW (or 4–5 hours on HIGH).

2. Just before serving, prepare the salsa: stir together all salsa ingredients in a small serving bowl.

3. Stir chili and serve, topping each portion with about 2 tablespoons of the salsa.

1 (28-ounce) can crushed tomatoes

1 (15.5-ounce) can small red beans

1 (15.5-ounce) can small white beans

1 (15.5-ounce) can black beans, drained

1 (12-ounce) jar roasted red peppers, drained and chopped

1 medium onion, finely chopped

1 yellow bell pepper, finely chopped

½ jalapeño, seeded and finely chopped, or more to taste

2 tablespoons GF Chili Powder (page 200)

2 tablespoons olive oil

2 tablespoons whole-grain cornmeal

2 teaspoons minced garlic

2 teaspoons vegetable bouillon (such as Organic Better than Bouillon®)

1½ teaspoons cumin

1 teaspoon oregano

½ teaspoon kosher salt or more to taste

⅛ teaspoon crushed red pepper flakes or more to taste

For the avocado salsa

2 ripe avocados, chopped

½ cup finely chopped fresh cilantro

2 tablespoons fresh lime juice

Easy Vegetable Dal

Serves 8 (about 1⅓ cups each)

DAIRY-FREE

1 cup red lentils, rinsed

¾ millet or quinoa

1 (32-ounce) package vegetable broth (such as Pacific Natural Foods®)

1 (28-ounce) can diced tomatoes

1 (13.5-ounce) can coconut milk (regular or light)

1 (15-ounce) can chickpeas, rinsed and drained

1 onion, thinly sliced

1 carrot, peeled and finely chopped

¼ cup currants

2 tablespoon grated fresh ginger

2 tablespoon tomato paste

1 tablespoon lemon juice

1 tablespoon olive oil

2 teaspoons minced garlic

2 teaspoons ground cumin

2 teaspoons ground turmeric

2 teaspoons curry powder

1¼ teaspoon kosher salt

½ teaspoon ground black pepper

¼ teaspoon ground coriander

⅛ teaspoon cayenne pepper or more to taste

1 (5-ounce) package baby spinach, finely chopped

¼ cup finely chopped fresh cilantro or thinly sliced scallions

The word *dal* comes from the Sanskrit, meaning "to split." All Indian dal recipes use split peas, beans, or lentils, spices, tomatoes, and onions to make a stew-like mixture that's frequently served with rice (we use basmati). Our dal also incorporates millet or quinoa for extra protein, and as a result the mixture is a bit thicker than most. Don't be intimidated by the relatively long ingredient list—this recipe is truly easy, and one of Kimberly's favorite meatless meals. Enjoy it for dinner; then freeze the leftovers for lunches that reheat beautifully.

1. Stir together the lentils and millet in the slow cooker crock; set aside.

2. Stir together all the remaining ingredients except the spinach and cilantro in a large bowl. Add the mixture to the crock; do not stir. Cover and cook 8–10 hours on LOW (or 4–5 hours on HIGH). Stir well. Test the doneness of the lentils; they should be tender and cooked through.

3. Add the spinach into the dal and stir until it is wilted. Garnish each bowl with a bit of cilantro.

TECHNIQUE TIP To enhance the flavor of the spices, briefly sauté them in the olive oil before adding them to the dal mixture.

New England–Style Baked Beans

DAIRY-FREE

Serves 8 (about ⅔ cup each)

Bring these traditional baked beans (minus the salt pork) to your next potluck and the crock will be empty before you blink. For a meatless dinner, serve these beans with homemade cornbread (page 188) drizzled with maple syrup and Classic Coleslaw (page 190). As in most baked bean recipes, the beans are precooked before being cooked again in sauce (see Technique Tip below).

1. Add the beans to the slow cooker crock and cover them with at least 2 inches of water. Cover and cook 8 hours on LOW (or 4 hours on HIGH).

2. Drain the beans and return them to the crock. Add the remaining ingredients to the crock and stir well. Cover and cook 8 hours on LOW (or 4 hours on HIGH). If possible, stir the beans once during the cooking. If not possible, do not worry; the beans will be perfectly okay.

3. Stir beans well before serving. These are thickly sauced, richly flavored beans. Add a bit more water or vegetable broth to thin the sauce to your liking.

TECHNIQUE TIP When preparing beans cooked in sweet or acidic liquids, the beans should be cooked beforehand or they will harden in the cooking liquid. After much trial and error, we found that cooking the beans overnight and then beginning the actual recipe the next morning works best.

1 pound dried small white beans, rinsed and picked over

1 onion, finely chopped

2 cups vegetable broth (such as Pacific Natural Foods®)

¾ cup ketchup

¼ cup molasses

¼ cup real maple syrup or honey

¼ cup brown sugar

2 tablespoons cider vinegar

1 tablespoon Bragg Liquid Aminos®

1 tablespoon canola oil

1 tablespoon dry mustard

1 tablespoon minced garlic

1¼ teaspoons kosher salt

1 teaspoon smoked paprika

¼ teaspoon ground black pepper

pinch ground cloves (optional)

Tuscan White Beans with Tomatoes and Sage

Serves 5 (about 1½ cups each)

A traditional side dish in Italy, these hearty beans easily translate into a vegetarian main course. Pair them with a nice green salad and Parmesan Herb Cornbread (page 189). Tuscan White Beans are great for batch cooking because they freeze and reheat nicely.

1 pound dried small white beans, picked over, soaked overnight or quick-soaked (see page 25 for soaking instructions)

2 cups water

1 (28-ounce) can whole tomatoes

¼ cup good-quality extra-virgin olive oil

5 cloves garlic, thinly sliced

2 sprigs fresh sage with at least 5 leaves each

1 shallot, thinly sliced

1½ teaspoons kosher salt

pinch crushed red pepper

1. Stir together all ingredients in the slow cooker crock. Cover and cook 10–12 hours on LOW (or 6 hours on HIGH).

2. Stir well, test doneness of beans (they should be tender), and discard sprigs of sage. Leave tomatoes whole or crush them with the back of a wooden spoon if you like.

Layered Mediterranean Casserole

Serves 6 (about 1½ cups each)

This colorful casserole makes use of a summer garden's bounty (plus a few pantry staples). Don't let the ingredient lists scare you—once you've done the prep work, the whole thing comes together quickly and cooks in just 3 hours. Gluten-free pitas make a great go-with for this dish.

1. Brush the olive oil all over the inside of the slow cooker crock (leave excess in crock). Layer the vegetables in the crock, starting with the zucchini on the bottom, followed by half the red peppers (set aside remaining peppers), and ending with the leeks. Set aside.

2. Prepare the bean layer: Stir together all the ingredients for the bean layer except the olives and broth in a medium mixing bowl until evenly combined. Spoon the bean mixture over the leeks in the crock; spread with a spatula to make an even layer. Place reserved peppers over the top of the bean layer; then sprinkle with olives. Pour the broth over the top (do not stir).

3. Cover and cook 3 hours on LOW. Remove lid and let casserole rest 5 minutes before serving. To serve, garnish by sprinkling the feta over the top, followed by the chopped fresh tomato and basil.

For the vegetable layer

2 tablespoons olive oil

2 medium zucchini, halved, seeded, and thinly sliced (about 3 cups)

2 red bell peppers, seeded, thinly sliced, divided

1 large leek, trimmed, washed well, and thinly sliced

For the bean layer

2 (15-ounce) cans cannellini beans, drained and rinsed

1 (14-ounce) can quartered artichoke hearts, drained

¾ cup prepared pesto (such as Classico® Traditional Basil Pesto)

½ cup chopped, soft sun-dried tomatoes

1 large shallot, chopped

2 cloves garlic, minced

3 tablespoons minced, fresh oregano leaves (or 1½ teaspoons dry)

2 tablespoons minced, fresh thyme leaves (or 1 teaspoon dry)

2 tablespoons capers, drained and minced

½ teaspoon ground black pepper

½ teaspoon garlic salt

½ cup pitted Greek olives, halved

½ cup vegetable broth (such as Pacific Natural Foods®)

For the garnish

1½ cups crumbled feta cheese

1 medium tomato, chopped

⅓ cup sliced, fresh basil leaves

Buckwheat (Kasha) and Green Bean Casserole

Serves 10 (about ½ cup each)

This vegetarian casserole is a healthier take on the traditional green bean casserole. It is a fantastic dish to serve on holidays and bring to potlucks. Sautéed mushrooms and shallots give the dish its signature flavor, and toasted almonds step in for the traditional fried onions.

1 tablespoon butter

2 shallots, finely chopped

1 teaspoon minced garlic

8 ounces white mushrooms, coarsely chopped

1 teaspoon kosher salt

½ teaspoon ground black pepper

2¼ cups vegetable broth (such as Pacific Natural Foods®)

1 cup kasha (roasted buckwheat), rinsed

1 tablespoon Bragg Liquid Aminos®

1 pound frozen, French cut green beans, thawed

⅔ cup half-and-half

½ cup toasted sliced almonds

1. Warm the butter in a large nonstick skillet over medium heat. When hot, add the shallots, garlic, mushrooms, salt, and pepper. Cook and stir mushrooms for about 10 minutes (they will give off a lot of liquid and brown up nicely).

2. Stir together the mushroom mixture, broth, kasha, and Bragg Liquid Aminos in the slow cooker crock. Cover and cook 2 hours on HIGH.

3. Stir in the beans and half-and-half. Cover and cook an additional 10 minutes on HIGH. Serve the casserole family-style, garnished with toasted almonds.

INGREDIENT INFO Buckwheat can be purchased in two forms. We prefer the nutty taste of kasha, which is roasted buckwheat, to that of unroasted buckwheat, also known as groats. We have had good luck finding both types in natural food stores and even in some large grocery stores.

Butternut Squash Risotto

Serves 4 (about 1½ cups each)

When you're living gluten-free, rice is a staple, so enjoying many different kinds of rice dishes makes good sense. Risotto is an Italian dish made with arborio rice. When traditionally prepared, risotto is cooked on the stove-top with lots of stirring. Slow-cooked risotto only requires a tiny bit of sautéing; other than that, the slow cooker does all the work.

1. Heat oil in a medium nonstick skillet over medium heat. When hot, add the shallots, garlic, sage, salt, pepper, and nutmeg. Cook and stir until the shallots soften, about 4 minutes. Transfer the shallot mixture to the slow cooker. Add the rice and stir to coat with the seasonings.

2. Stir in 3½ cups of the broth, Bragg Liquid Aminos, and lemon juice. Top mixture with the squash; do not stir. Cover and cook 2 hours on HIGH. The rice should be tender and most of the liquid should be absorbed.

3. Add cream, ½ cup of the Parmesan cheese, and remaining ½ cup broth to the crock and stir until risotto is evenly blended.

4. Garnish each bowl of risotto with a bit of the remaining Parmesan, freshly ground pepper, and fresh sage leaves, if desired.

2 tablespoons olive oil

3 shallots, finely chopped

1 teaspoon minced garlic

1 tablespoon finely chopped fresh sage or 1 teaspoon dried sage

1 teaspoon kosher salt or more to taste

⅛ teaspoon ground black pepper

generous pinch ground nutmeg

1¼ cups arborio rice

1 (32-ounce) package vegetable broth (such as Pacific Natural Foods®), divided

1 tablespoon Bragg Liquid Aminos®

1 tablespoon lemon juice

1 (16-ounce) package frozen butternut squash, thawed

¼ cup heavy cream

⅔ cup grated Parmesan cheese, divided

freshly ground black pepper (optional)

fresh sage sprigs (optional)

TECHNIQUE TIP Leftover risotto can be made into crispy risotto cakes. Season some gluten-free bread crumbs with a touch of GF Seasoning Salt (page 199). Form the refrigerated risotto into 4-inch patties. Press both sides into the seasoned bread crumbs. Fry cakes in a little oil until crispy and heated through. Delish!

Slow-Cooked Polenta

Serves 12 (about ½ cup each)

Cookbook author Paula Wolfert changed the painstaking process of preparing polenta when she introduced the world to oven-baked polenta (cheers of "No more stirring!" could be heard around the world). We've adapted her concept to slow cooking (making it even easier on the cook). Adding cream and Parmesan cheese to our recipe makes a polenta that is not exactly authentic, but it is perfectly delicious. This soft, creamy dish is the perfect accompaniment for braised or grilled meats. For a vegetarian option, pair it with Summer Vegetable and Tomato Sauce (page 104) and some sautéed portabellas.

5½ cups chicken or vegetable broth (such as Pacific Natural Foods®)

2 cups whole-grain cornmeal

⅓ cup grated Parmesan cheese

¼ cup heavy cream

2 tablespoons olive oil

1½ teaspoons kosher salt

pinch ground cayenne pepper

1. Add all the ingredients to the slow cooker crock and stir well. Cover and cook 5 hours on LOW (or 2½ hours on HIGH).

2. Stir well until polenta is evenly blended and creamy.

Caponata

Serves 16 (about ½ cup each)

Traditionally served as one component of an antipasti plate in Italy, caponata can easily become a sauce to serve over white beans, rice, or your favorite gluten-free pasta. There are countless variations of this sweet and tangy classic dish.

1. Put the eggplant cubes in a large colander and toss with salt; let sit for 1 hour. Rinse the eggplant well. Using a clean kitchen towel or a few layers of paper towels, gently press down on the eggplant to squeeze out any excess water.

2. While eggplant is being salted, add the tomatoes, onion, pine nuts, currants, olive oil, tomato paste, balsamic vinegar, garlic, sugar, crushed red pepper, black pepper, and thyme to the slow cooker crock. Stir to combine.

3. Once the eggplant is rinsed and pressed dry, add it to the other ingredients and stir well. Cook 7–8 hours on LOW (or 3½–4 hours on HIGH).

4. To finish the caponata, stir in the fresh herbs and red wine vinegar. Season to taste. If necessary, add a touch more salt and crushed red pepper. Caponata may be served hot or at room temperature.

TECHNIQUE TIP You might be tempted to skip the eggplant salting step (step 1), but don't! The salt pulls water out of the eggplant, thereby preventing a watery mixture.

2 medium eggplants, peeled and cut into 1½-inch cubes

2 tablespoons kosher salt

2 (14.5-ounce) cans diced tomatoes, drained

1 red onion, thinly sliced

⅓ cup pine nuts

⅓ cup dried currants

¼ cup extra-virgin olive oil

2 tablespoons tomato paste

2 tablespoons balsamic vinegar

1 tablespoon minced garlic

2 teaspoons sugar

½ teaspoon crushed red pepper flakes or more to taste

½ teaspoon ground black pepper

½ teaspoon dried thyme

¼ cup finely chopped fresh mint

⅓ cup thinly sliced fresh basil

1 tablespoon red wine vinegar

Summer Vegetable and Tomato Sauce

Serves 10 (about ½ cup each)

¼ cup olive oil

3 cups thinly sliced summer squash
(zucchini, crookneck,
or a combination of both)

3 cups fresh tomatoes,
seeded and chopped

½ pound fresh green beans,
cut into 1-inch pieces

1 medium onion, finely chopped

1 large carrot, finely chopped

5 cloves garlic, minced

1 (6-ounce) can tomato paste

⅓ cup red wine

½ cup water

2 teaspoons dried oregano leaves
(or 2 tablespoons fresh
oregano leaves)

2 teaspoons kosher salt

½ teaspoon garlic salt

¼ teaspoon ground black pepper

½ cup half-and-half (optional)

½ cup chopped parsley

2 tablespoons chopped, fresh basil

¼ teaspoon Tabasco®

Bursting with fresh vegetables, this versatile sauce can easily be tailored to utilize your summer garden's bounty. Serve the sauce in the customary way—over your favorite gluten-free pasta—or ladle it over a grilled chicken breast. It's also delicious as a condiment for scrambled eggs. Omit the cream if you want to go dairy-free or are watching calories.

1. Brush the inside of the slow cooker crock with olive oil (leave excess in crock). Add and stir together the remaining ingredients except for the half-and-half (if using), parsley, basil, and hot sauce. Cover and cook 6 hours on LOW (or 3 hours on HIGH).

2. Just before serving, stir in the half-and-half, if desired, and the herbs and hot sauce.

Dairy-Free Variation

Omit half-and-half.

> **TECHNIQUE TIP** In this recipe (as in a few others in this book), we've specified an exact cooking time as opposed to a range of time, as we usually do. The reason is to keep some texture in the vegetables. Cooking the sauce another hour won't ruin it, but the vegetables will be softer (and less identifiable) and the sauce won't have as much texture.

9
Seafood

Recipe Variation
DAIRY-FREE

Greek Shrimp and Rice Casserole

Serves 4 (about 1½ cups each)

Greek flavors are a big hit with our families, so we're always looking for ways to switch up our usual Mediterranean-inspired dishes and this casserole nailed it for us. It's warm and comforting like a casserole should be, but not at all humdrum like many casseroles we've come across. Plus, it doesn't take long to cook, making it perfect for weekend cooking or even as a brunch entree. Feel free to add more spinach if you like, and if you've got leftover rice, this is the place to use it. We like to serve this with a simple tomato salad.

1 (8-ounce) bottle clam juice

1 tablespoon olive oil

1 tablespoon freshly squeezed lemon juice

2 cloves garlic, minced

1½ teaspoons dried oregano

1 teaspoon kosher salt

¼ teaspoon ground black pepper

1 ¼ pounds jumbo (21–25) raw shrimp, peeled, deveined, and tails removed

2 cups cooked white or brown rice (or an 8.8-ounce package microwave-ready plain rice)

½ (6-ounce) package baby spinach

½ cup feta cheese (optional)

¼ cup pitted, sliced kalamata olives

2 tablespoons chopped fresh Italian parsley

1. Stir together the first seven ingredients (clam juice through pepper) in the slow cooker crock. Add the shrimp and stir to coat the shrimp with the liquid. Cover and cook 1½ hours on LOW.

2. Stir in the rice, cover, and cook another 1 hour on LOW.

3. Just before serving, stir in the spinach, feta, and olives. Divide casserole between plates and garnish with the parsley.

Dairy-Free Variation

Omit the feta cheese.

Shrimp and Scallop Thai Curry

Serves 6 (about 1⅓ cups each)

Make Thai take-out at home with this easy recipe. As for most of our seafood recipes, the cooking time is short. Kimberly loves to make this for Friday night dinner (served over jasmine or brown rice). Start it when the kids get home from school, and by the time the "I'm starving!" cries start, dinner is ready!

1. Stir together the first 11 ingredients (onion through lime zest) in the slow cooker crock. Cover and cook 3 hours on LOW (or 1½ hours on HIGH).

2. Add the shrimp and scallops to the crock and stir well. Stir in the bell pepper and spinach. Cover and cook another 2 hours on LOW (or 1 hour on HIGH). Stir in lime juice and scallions. Garnish each serving with peanuts and cilantro. Offer sriracha on the side, if desired.

Fish Variation

Replace the shrimp and scallops with 1I pounds of firm, boneless fish fillets, such as **cod or halibut**, cut into 2-inch pieces.

> **INGREDIENT INFO** Sriracha sauce is a spicy, Thai chili sauce that is readily available in most grocery stores. If you cannot find it, simply substitute another hot sauce.

1 onion, thinly sliced

1 cup julienne-cut carrots

1 (14-ounce) can coconut milk (regular or light)

½ cup bottled clam juice

2 tablespoons quick-cooking tapioca

1 tablespoon brown sugar

1 tablespoon fish sauce (such as Thai Kitchen®)

1 tablespoon grated fresh ginger

1 tablespoon minced garlic

2 teaspoons bottled Thai red or green curry paste (such as Thai Kitchen®) or more to taste

1 teaspoon lime zest

1 pound large shrimp, peeled, deveined, and tails removed

¾ pound sea scallops

1 red bell pepper, thinly sliced

1 (5-ounce) bag baby spinach, coarsely chopped

1 tablespoon fresh lime juice

3 scallions, thinly sliced

3 tablespoons finely chopped peanuts

2 tablespoons finely chopped cilantro

Sriracha chili sauce or other hot sauce (optional)

Moroccan-Spiced Halibut

Serves 4

Moroccan food typically contains a wide variety of spices. It's richly flavored, zesty, but not spicy (hot) per se. For this recipe we used halibut steaks, which yield two servings per steak, but you could also use four halibut fillets. This recipe would also be suitable for cod fillets and even salmon. Either way, serve the fish with brown rice couscous (such as Lundberg®), or basmati rice and a side of sautéed vegetables.

For the marinade

4 cloves garlic, minced

2 tablespoons fresh lemon juice

2 tablespoons olive oil

1 tablespoon paprika

1 teaspoon cumin

¾ teaspoon kosher salt

½ teaspoon ground coriander

¼ teaspoon turmeric

¼ teaspoon cayenne pepper

For the fish

*2 (12-ounce) halibut steaks
    (or 1½ pounds halibut fillets)*

½ cup chopped cilantro (for garnish)

1. Add the marinade ingredients to a large zip-top bag. Place the halibut steaks in the bag, making sure that the marinade has coated both sides of the fish. Refrigerate for 4–6 hours.

2. Add 2 tablespoons water to the slow cooker crock. Remove the fish from the bag and place it in the crock. Cover and cook 1½–2 hours on LOW. When done, let fish sit, uncovered, for 5 minutes before serving.

3. Use a spatula to remove the steaks from the slow cooker and transfer them to a plate. Gently remove the bones from the steaks (they should all come out easily, usually in one piece). Flake the fish with a fork into bite-sized chunks, removing any visible skin. If using fillets, do not flake them into pieces.

4. To serve, divide fish between plates (serve it on top of couscous or rice for a nice presentation) and garnish each portion with a sprinkling of cilantro.

Smoked Paprika Salmon with Edamame and Quinoa Succotash

Serves 4 (1 piece fish and about 1½ cups vegetable mixture each)

Packed with protein and fiber, this meal-in-one delivers the nutrition you want and the flavors you love. Never cooked with edamame (soybeans)? This succotash mixture is an easy introduction because it utilizes shelled, frozen beans. Note that the succotash mixture is cooked first, and the fish is added later (and only cooks 1½ to 2 hours). Be sure to plan accordingly.

1. Layer the succotash ingredients into the slow cooker crock, starting with the quinoa on the bottom and ending with the clam juice. Do not stir. Cover and cook 4 hours on LOW (or 2 hours on HIGH).

2. While the succotash cooks, marinate the salmon: add the olive oil, lemon juice, garlic, and paprika to a gallon-sized zip-top plastic bag. Seal the bag and shake to combine the ingredients. Place the salmon fillets into the bag, reseal it, and flip to make sure the marinade coats the fish. Refrigerate until it's time to add the fish to the slow cooker.

3. Remove the salmon from the plastic bag and discard remaining marinade. Place the salmon on top of the succotash; do not stir. Cover and cook 1½–2 hours on LOW (or 45–60 minutes on HIGH).

4. Transfer the fillets to a platter. Stir succotash well and divide it between 4 plates. Place one fillet on each plate and garnish with parsley, if desired.

For the succotash

¼ cup quinoa

1 cup frozen, shelled edamame beans, thawed

1 celery stalk, finely chopped

2 scallions, thinly sliced

1½ teaspoon Italian seasoning

1 teaspoon kosher salt, divided

¼ teaspoon ground black pepper

1½ cups frozen corn, thawed

¾ cup chopped roasted red peppers

1 (14.5-ounce) can diced tomatoes

⅔ cup bottled clam juice or chicken broth (such as Pacific Natural Foods®)

For the fish

1 tablespoon olive oil

1 tablespoon lemon juice

1 teaspoon minced garlic

1 teaspoon smoked paprika

4 (6-ounce) salmon fillets, skinned

finely chopped fresh parsley (optional, for garnish)

DAIRY-FREE

Garlicky Salmon with Leeks and Wild Rice

Serves 4 (1 piece fish and 1⅓ cups rice and leek mixture each)

We're big fans of leeks, and this recipe combines them with flavorful salmon fillets and chewy wild rice for a filling and healthful meal. Wild rice takes a while to cook, but fish doesn't, so some separate cooking is required here. For best results, we recommend cooking this dish on the low setting to keep the fish moist. Round out your meal with steamed asparagus or green beans.

For the rice mixture

1 tablespoon butter

2 large leeks, trimmed, washed well, and thinly sliced

1 cup wild rice (not seasoned rice mix)

½ teaspoon kosher salt

1 (32-ounce) package vegetable broth (such as Pacific Natural Foods®)

For the marinade

4 cloves garlic, minced

2 tablespoons plus 2 teaspoons Bragg Liquid Aminos®

2 teaspoons vegetable oil

½ teaspoon onion powder

¼ teaspoon ground black pepper

For the fish

4 (6-ounce) salmon fillets, skinned

⅛ teaspoon paprika (optional garnish)

1. Coat the inside of the slow cooker crock with butter, leaving any extra in the crock. Add the leeks to the crock; top with rice. Sprinkle with salt; pour the broth over the top (no need to stir). Cover and cook 4 hours on LOW.

2. While the rice is cooking, prepare the salmon: Add the marinade ingredients to a large zip-top bag. Place the salmon in the bag, making sure that the marinade coats both sides of the fish pieces. Refrigerate for 4 hours while the rice cooks.

3. After the rice has cooked 4 hours, uncover the crock and stir to combine leeks and rice. Remove the salmon fillets from the bag and discard marinade. Place salmon on top of the rice mixture. Cover the crock and cook another 1½–2 hours on LOW. When done, let fish sit, uncovered, for 5 minutes before serving. To serve, use a spatula to remove the salmon fillets from the slow cooker and place on individual plates. Garnish each fish portion with a sprinkle of paprika, if desired. Stir the rice and leek mixture and divide it between the plates, spooning it alongside the salmon.

Dairy-Free Variation

Replace butter with olive oil.

INGREDIENT INFO   You've probably noticed leeks in the produce department; they basically look like scallions on steroids. Leeks are a member of the allium family of vegetables, which includes garlic, shallots, scallions, and onions. However, the leek has a much more subtle flavor than its cousins, making it suitable for eating raw (in salads, for example) or cooked.

Lemon Dill Salmon

Serves 4 (1 piece fish each)

This is a super-easy, foolproof way to prepare salmon. Since fish does not take very long to cook, it's best to make this on a day when you'll be sticking around the house. Leftovers, if there are any, are great for topping a salad. Leafy greens and red-skinned potatoes are nice accompaniments to the fish.

DAIRY-FREE

For the marinade

½ cup fresh lemon juice

1 tablespoon canola oil

2 teaspoons minced garlic

1 teaspoon dried dill
  (or 1 tablespoon fresh dill)

For the fish

4 (6-ounce) salmon fillets, skinned

½ teaspoon kosher salt

¼ teaspoon ground black pepper

fresh dill sprigs (optional, for garnish)

1. Add the marinade ingredients to a large zip-top bag. Place the salmon into the bag, making sure that the marinade coats both sides of the fish pieces. Refrigerate for 4–6 hours.

2. Remove salmon from the bag and place in the slow cooker crock (discard marinade). Sprinkle the fish with salt and pepper. Cover and cook 3 hours on LOW.

3. Let fish sit, uncovered, for 5 minutes before serving. Garnish each portion with a fresh dill sprig, if desired.

Recipe Variation
DAIRY-FREE

10
Poultry

INGREDIENT INFO
- Is poultry gluten-free? Yes, as long as brine containing hydrolyzed wheat protein has not been added to it during processing.
- "All-natural" poultry is usually unbrined and sold in its natural state, without any additives.
- "Certified organic" poultry has been raised without hormones and antibiotics. Organic poultry is usually sold without any additives. Organic poultry is also fed organic feed.
- "Free-range poultry" is allowed extra living space but is not necessarily organic or unbrined.
- As always, read the label on packaged poultry; if you are still unsure, ask the butcher.

Greek Chicken with Tomatoes, Rice, Feta, and Olives

Serves 4 (about 2 chicken thighs and 1 cup vegetable mixture each)

This aromatic dish features all the Greek flavors you'd expect, augmented with tender chicken and fresh herbs. Incorporating leftover cooked rice fills out the dish and is oh so convenient. If you have no cooked rice handy, use the precooked, plain rice sold at most markets.

2 (14.5-ounce) cans diced tomatoes, drained

½ medium onion, finely chopped

¼ cup chopped sun-dried tomatoes

2 tablespoons tomato paste

1 tablespoon lemon juice

2 teaspoons minced garlic

1½ teaspoons dried oregano

¾ teaspoon ground cumin

½ teaspoon kosher salt or more to taste

½ teaspoon ground black pepper

2 pounds boneless, skinless chicken thighs, trimmed of fat

2 cups cooked brown or white rice

¼ cup finely chopped parsley

¼ cup finely chopped mint

½ cup pitted kalamata olives, quartered lengthwise

½ cup feta cheese

1. Stir together the first 10 ingredients (diced tomatoes through black pepper) in the slow cooker crock.

2. Nestle chicken thighs into the mixture. Cover and cook 8 hours on LOW (or 4 hours on HIGH). At the end of cooking, use tongs to transfer thighs to a plate; cover with foil. Add rice, parsley, and mint to the tomato mixture. Stir well. Cover and cook for 5–10 minutes until the rice heats through.

3. Divide tomato and rice mixture between 4 shallow bowls; top each bowl with the cooked chicken, olives, and feta.

Dairy-Free Variation

Omit feta.

Chicken Cacciatore

DAIRY-FREE

Serves 4 (about 2 chicken thighs and 1 cup vegetable mixture each)

We've upgraded this Italian classic a bit by replacing the traditional green pepper and onion combination with Italian frying peppers, red bell peppers, and Vidalia onions. Serve this saucy cacciatore over steamed rice or your favorite gluten-free pasta. If you have a tough time finding Italian frying peppers, substitute Anaheim peppers or a yellow bell pepper.

1. Stir together tomatoes, wine, tomato paste, olive oil, garlic, oregano, paprika, kosher salt, and black pepper in a small mixing bowl; set aside.

2. Sprinkle the tapioca into the slow cooker crock. Add the onion and peppers to the crock; top with the chicken. Pour the seasoned tomato mixture over the chicken. Do not stir.

3. Cover and cook for 8 hours on LOW (or 4 hours on HIGH). Using tongs, transfer chicken thighs to plates. Stir the capers and sliced basil into the sauce in the crock. Spoon the sauce over each portion of chicken and garnish with fresh basil, if desired.

2 (14.5-ounce) cans diced tomatoes, drained

¼ cup dry red wine or dry white wine

3 tablespoons tomato paste

1 tablespoon extra-virgin olive oil

1 tablespoon minced garlic

2 teaspoons oregano

½ teaspoon paprika

½ teaspoon kosher salt or more to taste

¼ teaspoon ground black pepper

1 tablespoon quick-cooking tapioca

½ medium Vidalia onion, thinly sliced

1 red bell pepper, thinly sliced

2 Italian frying peppers (also called Cubanelle peppers), thinly sliced

2 pounds boneless, skinless chicken thighs, trimmed of fat

1 tablespoon drained capers, finely chopped

¼ cup fresh basil, thinly sliced

extra basil leaves for garnish (optional)

Moroccan Chicken with Potatoes and Carrots

Makes 4 servings

1/3 cup water

1 tablespoon olive oil

1 tablespoon grated fresh ginger

2 teaspoons chicken bouillon (such as Organic Better than Bouillon®)

2 teaspoon minced garlic

1½ teaspoon ground cumin

1 teaspoon turmeric

½ teaspoon dried thyme

½ teaspoon kosher salt, more to taste

½ teaspoon ground black pepper

¼ teaspoon ground coriander

⅛ teaspoon ground cinnamon

pinch cayenne pepper, more to taste

2 pounds boneless, skinless chicken thighs, trimmed of fat

4 medium red potatoes, halved

3 carrots, peeled, halved lengthwise, and cut into ½-inch pieces

1 medium onion, chopped

1/3 cup golden raisins

1/3 cup sliced salad olives, drained

1 lemon, thinly sliced

3 tablespoons finely chopped cilantro or mint leaves

1/3 cup Greek-style yogurt or sour cream (optional garnish)

This tender chicken recipe, heady with Moroccan spices like turmeric and ginger, is finished with a lemony sauce studded with olives and raisins.

1. Stir together the water, oil, ginger, bouillon, garlic, cumin, turmeric, thyme, salt, pepper, coriander, cinnamon, and cayenne pepper in a medium mixing bowl. Add 3 tablespoons of the mixture to the slow cooker crock. Add the chicken to the remaining spice mixture in the bowl and toss well to coat chicken with the seasonings.

2. Layer the vegetables in the crock, starting with the potatoes on the bottom and ending with the onion. Sprinkle the raisins over the onion. Top the vegetables with the chicken, scraping any remaining seasonings onto the chicken. Sprinkle the olives over the chicken, and arrange the lemon slices over all. Do not stir.

3. Cover and cook 8 hours on LOW (or 4 hours on HIGH). Using tongs, transfer the lemon slices to a small bowl. Using a fork, gently press the juice out of the lemons and add the juice back to the crock (discard the lemon slices).

4. Using a slotted spoon, divide potatoes and chicken between plates. Give the sauce a good stir and divide it between the plates, ladling it over the chicken. Garnish each plate with cilantro or mint and a dollop of yogurt, if desired.

Dairy-Free Variation

Omit the yogurt.

Four Seasons Chicken

Serves 4

Four Seasons pizza is one of the most popular pizzas in Italy, and we think it translates nicely to a chicken dish that's perfect for a busy weeknight. The artichokes represent spring, olives are for summer, earthy mushrooms are for fall, and prosciutto is for winter. This is a delicious chicken dish: the better quality the ingredients, the more flavorful the end results.

1. Warm the oil in a large nonstick skillet over medium heat. When hot, add the mushrooms. Cook and stir mushrooms for about 10 minutes (they will give off a lot of liquid and brown up nicely). While the mushrooms cook, add the garlic, bouillon, salt, oregano, black pepper, and red pepper to the skillet. When the mushrooms have finished cooking, stir in the tomato sauce and tomato paste. Turn off heat and set mixture aside.

2. Place the potatoes into the slow cooker crock, making an even layer. Top with even layers of artichoke hearts, then olives, chicken, and prosciutto. Top everything with an even layer of the mushroom sauce mixture. Do not stir. Cover and cook 8 hours on LOW (or 4 hours on HIGH).

3. Using tongs, divide chicken and potatoes between four plates or shallow bowls. Set aside 2 tablespoons of fresh basil for garnish. Stir the remaining basil and the mozzarella into the crock. To serve, spoon the sauce mixture over the chicken and potatoes, dividing it between portions. Garnish each plate with a bit of the reserved basil.

Dairy-Free Variation

Omit the mozzarella.

1 tablespoon olive oil

1 (16-ounce) package sliced white mushrooms

1 teaspoon minced garlic

1 teaspoon chicken bouillon (such as Organic Better than Bouillon®)

1 teaspoon kosher salt

1 teaspoon dried oregano

½ teaspoon ground black pepper

¼ teaspoon crushed red pepper

1 (15-ounce) can tomato sauce

3 tablespoons tomato paste

1 pound small red potatoes, halved

2 (14-ounce) cans artichoke quarters, drained

½ cup kalamata olives, quartered lengthwise

2 pounds boneless, skinless chicken thighs, trimmed of fat

3 ounces prosciutto di Parma, cut into thin strips

⅓ cup fresh basil, thinly sliced, divided

1 (8-ounce) fresh mozzarella ball, cut into small bite-sized pieces

Tex-Mex Chicken with Black Beans

Serves 4 (about 2 chicken thighs and 1 cup beans each)

Saucy black beans, tender chicken, and a sprinkle of cheese create a flavorful meal that everyone is sure to love. Plain white or brown rice makes a fine side dish.

2 tablespoons canola oil

2 tablespoons GF Chili Powder
(see page 200)

2 pounds boneless, skinless chicken
thighs, trimmed of fat

2 (15.5-ounce) cans black beans,
rinsed and drained

¾ cup canned crushed tomatoes

1 yellow bell pepper, finely chopped

½ onion, finely chopped

1 jalapeño, seeded and finely chopped

2 tablespoons tomato paste

1 tablespoon minced garlic

½ teaspoon kosher salt

½ teaspoon ground black pepper

1 cup crumbled feta cheese

2 tablespoons finely chopped cilantro
or thinly sliced scallions

1. Stir together the oil and chili powder in a medium mixing bowl. Transfer 1 tablespoon of the oil mixture to the slow cooker crock. Add the chicken thighs to the remaining spice mixture in the bowl. Toss until chicken is coated with spices; set aside.

2. Add the black beans, crushed tomatoes, bell pepper, onion, jalapeño, tomato paste, garlic, salt, and black pepper to the slow cooker crock and stir well.

3. Nestle the chicken thighs into the bean mixture. Cover and cook 8 hours on LOW (or 4 hours on HIGH).

4. To serve, transfer chicken thighs to plates. Stir the beans; then spoon them onto the plates. Garnish each plate with 1/4 cup feta and ½ tablespoon cilantro (or scallions).

Dairy-Free Variation

Omit the feta cheese.

INGREDIENT INFO *Queso fresco*, or "fresh cheese," has a tangy taste and crumbly texture. Although it is one of the most commonly used cheeses in Mexican cooking, *queso fresco* might not be easy to find at your market, which is why we called for the more widely available feta in this recipe. If you do happen to find *queso fresco*, give it a try!

Chicken Fajitas

Serves 6

This is the easiest way we've found to make flavorful fajitas, especially for a crowd. Serve them with your favorite gluten-free tortillas and the toppings of your choice (we're partial to shredded cheese and salsa).

1. Coat the inside of the slow cooker crock with cooking spray; set aside.

2. Add the spices (cayenne through black pepper) to a large, zip-top plastic bag; close bag and shake to combine. Add the chicken to the bag, reseal, and shake to coat the chicken with the spices.

3. Add the chicken to the crock; top with the onion and peppers. Cover and cook for 3 hours on LOW.

4. Using tongs, transfer the onions and peppers to a serving platter; set aside. Transfer the chicken to a cutting board and cut into ¼-inch strips with a sharp knife. Arrange chicken on the serving platter. Serve with tortillas and desired toppings.

Dairy-Free Variation

Omit cheese and sour cream toppings.

Nonstick cooking spray

1¼ teaspoons ground cayenne

1¼ teaspoons garlic salt

1 teaspoon ground cumin

1 teaspoon dried oregano leaves

1 teaspoon GF Chili Powder (see page 200)

½ teaspoon ground black pepper

2 pounds skinless, boneless, thin-sliced chicken breasts, fat trimmed

1 large Vidalia onion, sliced ¼-inch thick

1 red bell pepper, halved, seeded, and sliced ¼-inch thick

1 green bell pepper, halved, seeded, and sliced ¼-inch thick

Gluten-free tortillas

Toppings of your choice (salsa, sour cream, shredded cheese, etc.)

Cashew Chicken

Serves 4 (about 1¼ cups each)

Slightly sweet, slightly spicy, and packed with colorful peas and peppers, this restaurant favorite is easy to make at home in your slow cooker. Note the short cooking time and plan on being home since this recipe takes just a few hours. Serve it over hot rice and follow with fruit salad (we're partial to an easy mélange of pantry staples—drained mandarin oranges, drained pineapple chunks, and a sprinkle of shredded coconut) for a filling and healthy meal.

DAIRY-FREE

½ cup finely chopped sweet onion
   (about half a small onion)

½ cup chicken broth
   (such as Pacific Naturals®)

3 tablespoons Bragg Liquid Aminos®

2 tablespoons cornstarch

1 tablespoon rice vinegar

1 tablespoon minced garlic

2 teaspoons brown sugar

½ teaspoon kosher salt

½ teaspoon ground ginger

¼ teaspoon red pepper flakes

1½ pounds boneless, skinless chicken
   thighs, trimmed of fat

½ (4-ounce) package snow peas,
   cut in half on the diagonal

1 red or orange bell pepper,
   cut into ½-inch pieces

2 cups hot, cooked rice

2 scallions, chopped

½ cup salted cashews

1. Stir together the first 10 ingredients (onion through pepper flakes) in the slow cooker crock. Cut the chicken thighs into 1–2-inch chunks and add them to the mixture in the crock. Stir to coat the chicken with the sauce. Cover and cook 3 hours on LOW.

2. Add the snow peas and bell pepper to the chicken mixture. Stir well. Cover and cook another 30 minutes.

3. To serve, divide rice between bowls. Divide the chicken mixture between portions, spooning it over the rice. Garnish each portion with chopped scallions and about 2 tablespoons of the cashews.

Rosemary Chicken and Potatoes

DAIRY-FREE

Serves 4

Cooking a whole chicken in the slow cooker is a snap, and the result is moist, flavorful chicken that's fall-off-the-bone tender. We use small birds rather than big roasting chickens in our slow cooker recipes—they cook faster and fit better in most slow cookers. As a budget bonus, small birds are much more economical than roasting chickens.

1. Coat the inside of the slow cooker crock with cooking spray. Add wine and potatoes to the crock and set aside.

2. Stir together the olive oil, garlic, rosemary, salt, and pepper. Spoon a teaspoon of the mixture onto the potatoes and stir them to combine. Rub the remaining mixture over the chicken. Place the lemon half and garlic in the cavity of the bird. Place the chicken breast side down on the potatoes. Cover and cook 6–7 hours on LOW (or 3–3½ hours on HIGH). Check doneness with an instant-read thermometer (it should register 170°F at the thigh).

3. When done, remove lid and let chicken rest in the crock for 10 minutes. To serve, transfer chicken to a platter. Use a slotted spoon to scoop potatoes out of cooking liquid and arrange them around the chicken. (Alternatively, you could remove the skin from the chicken and slice the meat for serving—it will be very tender and practically fall off the bone.)

4. If desired, skim the fat from the cooking liquid and serve the liquid as "gravy" for the chicken. (Or refrigerate the cooking juices overnight; then skim off the fat and use the liquid as a flavorful soup base at a later date.)

---

nonstick cooking spray

¼ cup white wine

1½ pound mini gourmet potatoes (or larger, round potatoes cut into 1½-inch chunks)

2 tablespoons olive oil

1 tablespoon minced garlic

1 tablespoon dried rosemary, crushed between fingers

1 teaspoon kosher salt

¼ teaspoon black pepper

1 (4–5 pound) "all natural" chicken (giblets removed), rinsed and patted dry

½ lemon, pierced several times with a paring knife

1 large clove garlic, cut in half

Apple and Thyme Roasted Chicken with Apple Gravy

Serves 6

For the chicken

1 (28-ounce) bag mini gourmet potatoes (such as fingerling or Yukon Gold), washed well

¼ cup dry white wine or chicken broth (such as Pacific Naturals®)

1 tablespoon melted butter

1 tablespoon GF Seasoning Salt (see page 199)

1 ½ teaspoons dried thyme

¾ teaspoon paprika

½ teaspoon dry mustard

1 (4–5 pound) "all-natural" chicken (giblets removed), rinsed and patted dry

2 apples, peeled, cored, and quartered

½ onion

For the sauce

pan drippings

cooked apples from above list

cooked onion from above list

2 tablespoons cold butter, cut into small pieces

¼ teaspoon kosher salt or more to taste

⅛ teaspoon ground black pepper

⅛ teaspoon dried thyme

We love roasting whole chickens in our slow cookers! The subsequent leftovers are easily turned into chicken salad or chicken soup. The skin of slow-cooked chicken will not crisp up like it does in the oven, so we generally discard it before slicing the ultra-tender meat. Serve this chicken dish with steamed green beans or peas for a complete meal.

1. Add the potatoes and wine to the slow cooker crock; set aside.

2. Mix the butter, seasoning salt, thyme, paprika, and mustard in a small bowl until blended. Rub 1 teaspoon of the spice mixture into the chicken cavity. Rub remaining spices all over the chicken.

3. Place the chicken, breast side down, into the crock. Insert 1 apple quarter and the onion into the cavity. Place remaining apple pieces around the chicken. Cover and cook 6–7 hours on LOW (or 3–3½ hours on HIGH). The internal temperature of the chicken at the thigh should be 170°F.

4. When done, transfer the bird to a platter or cutting board and let it rest for 10 minutes. Using tongs, transfer the potatoes to a serving bowl.

5. To make the sauce: Remove the onion from the cavity of the chicken and add it back to the crock. Use an immersion blender to process the apples, onion, and chicken cooking juices into a very smooth sauce. Alternatively, a blender can be used for this task. Stir the butter, salt, pepper, and thyme into the sauce.

6. Remove the skin from the chicken and slice the chicken for serving. The meat will be very juicy and practically falling off the bone. Serve chicken with the potatoes and the apple gravy on the side.

Roasted Chicken
with Apricot and Fig Sauce

Serves 4

The figs add a little exotic flair to this roasted chicken, making it fancy enough for a Sunday supper but simple enough for weeknight fare. Barr's Green Beans Almondine (see page 195) and mashed potatoes are good companions for this delicious roasted chicken.

For the sauce

1 cup apricot preserves, divided

24 dried figs, halved, with stems removed (about 8 ounces)

2 shallots, thinly sliced

2 tablespoons apple cider vinegar

1 tablespoon Bragg Liquid Aminos®

For the chicken

1 (4–5 pound) whole "all-natural" chicken (giblets removed), rinsed and patted dry

2 tablespoons butter, melted

2 tablespoon brown sugar

1 teaspoons ginger

¼ teaspoon kosher salt

¼ teaspoon ground black pepper

1. Stir together ¼ cup of the preserves and all other sauce ingredients in the slow cooker crock. If desired, remove the skin from the chicken now. Place the chicken in the crock on top of the sauce, breast side up.

2. In a separate bowl, stir together the remaining ingredients. Brush the seasoning mixture onto the bird. Cover and cook 6–7 hours on LOW (or 3–3½ hours on HIGH). Check doneness with an instant-read thermometer (it should register 170°F at the thigh).

3. When done, transfer chicken to a platter, cover with foil, and let rest for 10 minutes before serving. Skim and discard any visible fat from the cooking juices in the crock. Add the remaining ¾ cup preserves to the crock and stir well.

4. Slice the chicken and serve the sauce on the side.

Dairy-Free Variation

Replace butter with olive oil.

Turkey Thighs with White Beans, Spinach, and Sage

Serves 4 (1 turkey thigh and about 1 cup bean and spinach mixture)

This recipe is really eight recipes in one. It can be made with turkey or chicken, accented with sage or rosemary, and finished with spinach or tomatoes.

1. Coat the slow cooker crock with cooking spray. Stir together the beans, leek, garlic, and red pepper in the crock. Place the turkey thighs on top of the bean mixture—do not stir. Set the crock aside.

2. In a separate bowl, whisk together the olive oil, wine, 1 tablespoon of the sage, lemon zest, garlic, salt, paprika, and pepper. Spoon this mixture over the turkey. Use the back of the spoon to spread the seasonings evenly over the turkey.

3. Cover and cook 8 hours on LOW (or 4 hours on HIGH).

4. Use tongs to transfer the turkey to a platter; the meat will be falling off the bone. Discard the bones. Cover the turkey with foil.

5. Add remaining tablespoon of sage, spinach, and Parmesan to the beans and stir well. The spinach will wilt and the mixture will thicken slightly as the Parmesan melts.

6. To serve, divide bean and spinach mixture between 4 shallow bowls; top each bowl with an equal amount of turkey. Garnish each bowl with fresh sage leaves or rosemary sprigs, if desired.

Dairy-Free Variation

Omit the Parmesan.

Nonstick cooking spray

2 (15.5-ounce) cans white beans, rinsed and drained

1 leek, washed well, halved lengthwise, and thinly sliced

½ teaspoon minced garlic

⅛ teaspoon crushed red pepper

4 turkey thighs, skin removed (or 2 pounds boneless, skinless chicken thighs)

2 tablespoons olive oil

2 tablespoon dry white wine

2 tablespoons thinly sliced fresh sage (or 2 tablespoons finely chopped fresh rosemary), divided

1½ teaspoons lemon zest

1½ teaspoons minced garlic

¾ teaspoon kosher salt

¼ teaspoon sweet or smoked paprika

¼ teaspoon ground black pepper

1 (5-ounce) package baby spinach, coarsely chopped (or 1 pint grape tomatoes, halved)

⅓ cup grated Parmesan cheese

Fresh sage leaves (optional)

Fresh rosemary sprigs (optional)

Garlic and Herb Roasted Turkey Breast
with Gluten-Free Gravy

Serves 6–8, depending on appetites

We love this classic turkey breast for a special weekend dinner (or even Thanksgiving). Mashed potatoes and Barr's Green Beans Almondine (page 195) are perfect companions. With all the delicious cooking juices, you'll discover that making gluten-free gravy is not as tough as you might think. Our favorite gravy recipe is offered opposite.

Nonstick cooking spray

1 (6–7 pound) turkey breast, rinsed and patted dry

½ onion

½ lemon

1 bay leaf

4 cloves garlic

¼ cup dry white wine

2 tablespoons butter, melted

1½ teaspoons minced garlic

1 tablespoon Italian seasoning

½ teaspoon paprika

½ teaspoon kosher salt

¼ teaspoon ground black pepper

1. Coat the slow cooker crock with cooking spray; set aside.

2. Remove the skin from the turkey breast, if desired. Place the turkey breast in the crock. (Ideally, the turkey should be breast side up, but the shape of your slow cooker crock may require the turkey be cooked on its side, and that is fine.) Place the onion, lemon, bay leaf, and garlic cloves into the cavity of the turkey breast.

3. Pour the white wine over the turkey. In a separate bowl, whisk together the butter, minced garlic, Italian seasoning, paprika, salt, and pepper. Brush the seasonings all over the turkey breast. Cover and cook 8 hours on LOW (or 4 hours on HIGH).

4. Transfer the turkey to a platter and tent with foil. Let the turkey rest at least 10 minutes before slicing. Reserve the cooking juices to make the gravy (recipe follows).

Dairy-Free Variation

Replace butter with olive oil.

Gluten-Free Gravy

This same gravy can be used as a sauce for turkey shepherd's pie. It is a good recipe to have in your files, especially around the holidays. You can substitute an equal amount of gluten-free turkey broth (such as Pacific Natural Brand®) for the cooking juices.

1. Strain cooking juices through a fine mesh sieve and discard solids. Skim any visible fat from the surface of the juices and discard. Set aside strained juices. You should have about 2⅓ cups.

2. Heat the butter over medium heat in a medium saucepan. When butter is melted and very frothy, whisk in the cornstarch and continue to cook until the mixture turns a golden brown, about 1 minute.

3. Whisk in the reserved cooking juices; the mixture will thicken as it comes to a boil. Keep whisking to prevent lumps.

4. Add the Gravy Master, salt, and pepper. Once the mixture has boiled and thickened, remove it from the heat. Taste and adjust seasonings if necessary.

cooking juices
2 tablespoons butter
3 tablespoons cornstarch
¼ teaspoon Gravy Master®
¼ teaspoon kosher salt
⅛ teaspoon ground black pepper, to taste

Dairy-Free Variation

Replace butter with Earth Balance® Vegan Buttery Sticks.

Cranberry Roasted Turkey Breast

Serves 6–8, depending on appetites

We love this turkey breast year-round—it's moist and flavorful, yet requires minimal effort. If you are expecting a big crowd for Thanksgiving, consider making this recipe in addition to your oven-roasted bird—it uses no oven space and also ensures that you'll have plenty of breast meat for everyone.

Nonstick cooking spray

1 tablespoon quick-cooking tapioca

1 cup dried cranberries

2 tablespoons butter

1 shallot, thinly sliced

½ teaspoon kosher salt

¼ teaspoon dried thyme

¼ teaspoon ground black pepper

1 teaspoon red wine vinegar

1 (14-ounce) can whole berry cranberry sauce, divided

1 (6–7 pound) turkey breast, rinsed and patted dry

1. Coat the slow cooker crock with cooking spray. Sprinkle the tapioca and dried cranberries over the bottom of the crock; set aside.

2. Heat the butter in a small saucepan over medium heat. When hot, add the shallot, salt, thyme, and black pepper. Cook and stir until shallot is soft and fragrant, about 5 minutes. Add the vinegar and ¼ cup of the cranberry sauce; stir to heat through. Set aside remaining cranberry sauce.

3. Remove the skin from the turkey breast, if desired. Place the turkey breast in the crock. (Ideally, the turkey should be breast side up, but the shape of your slow cooker may require the turkey be cooked on its side, and that is fine.) Pour the shallot and cranberry mixture over the turkey. Cover and cook 8 hours on LOW (or 4 hours on HIGH).

4. Transfer the turkey to a platter and tent with foil. Let the turkey rest at least 10 minutes before slicing. Skim and discard any visible fat from the cooking juices in the crock. Add the reserved cranberry sauce to the crock and stir well.

5. Slice the turkey breast and serve the sauce on the side.

Dairy-Free Variation

Replace butter with olive oil.

TECHNIQUE TIP   If you are a frugal cook or prefer the taste of homemade turkey broth to that of store-bought, you can make some turkey stock from leftover bones. Place the turkey carcass into the slow cooker with a sliced onion, a few carrots, a couple of garlic cloves, and a couple of stalks of celery. Pour enough water over the bones to just cover them. Season the liquid with dried thyme, salt, and ground black pepper. Cover and cook 10 hours on LOW (or 5 hours on HIGH). Discard the bones. Use a slotted spoon to discard the other large ingredients. Pour the broth through a fine mesh strainer and refrigerate. Once the broth is chilled, it is easy to skim any visible fat from the surface. Keep the broth refrigerated for up to a week, or freeze it for future use.

11
Pork

Recipe Variation
DAIRY-FREE

Potato, Ham, and Leek Casserole

Serves 4 (about 1½ cups each)

Ham and potatoes together make an über-comforting entrée. We think our recipe is all the better with the addition of leeks, though if you prefer regular onions, feel free to swap in a small, thinly sliced onion.

1 tablespoon butter, softened

2 pounds round, white potatoes, peeled and sliced ¼-inch thick

1 medium leek, trimmed, washed well, and sliced into ¼-inch pieces

8 ounces ham, cubed (such as Hormel Natural Choice®)

¼ cup chicken broth (such as Pacific Natural Foods®)

For the sauce

1¼ cups two-percent milk

1 tablespoon cornstarch

¼ teaspoon ground black pepper

¼ teaspoon celery salt

⅛ teaspoon ground nutmeg

1 cup shredded Gruyère cheese

1. Coat the inside of the slow cooker crock with the butter, leaving any extra in the crock. Stir together the potatoes and leeks in the crock; top with the ham cubes.

2. Pour broth over the potato mixture. Cover and cook 3½ hours on LOW.

3. Leave the slow cooker on LOW while preparing the sauce: Whisk together the milk, cornstarch, pepper, celery salt, and nutmeg in a microwavable bowl. Microwave the sauce mixture for 3 minutes on HIGH power; then whisk again. Return sauce to the microwave and continue to microwave another 2–3 minutes on HIGH power, whisking after each minute. Sauce will bubble up and thicken.

4. Remove sauce from microwave; stir in the Gruyère. Pour sauce over the potato mixture and stir to coat all ingredients with sauce. Cover and cook an additional half hour on LOW.

Scalloped Potatoes and Ham Variation

IN STEP 4: Omit the Gruyère and add ⅛ teaspoon kosher salt to the sauce mixture.

TECHNIQUE TIP Milk products tend to break down and appear curdled when cooked for a long time in the slow cooker. To avoid this, our recipe utilizes a white sauce prepared quickly in the microwave, then stirred into the potato mixture during the last half hour of cooking time.

Southern-Style Barbecue Ribs

Serves 6–8, depending on appetites

Southern-style pork ribs (also called country-style pork ribs) are cut from the shoulder region of the pig and generally have a lot of meat on them. This simple treatment combined with a long, slow cooking results in tender and flavorful ribs.

1. Stir together the first 5 ingredients (onion through vinegar) in the slow cooker crock; set aside.

2. In a separate bowl, stir together the next 10 ingredients (brown sugar through cayenne). Generously coat the ribs with this mixture and set them in the crock. Sprinkle any remaining spices over the ribs. Cover and cook 8–10 hours on LOW (or 4–5 hours on HIGH).

3. To serve, transfer ribs to a serving platter and cover with foil. Skim and discard any visible fat from the surface of the cooking juices. Stir the juices and spoon some of the juices over the ribs before serving.

1 sweet onion, thinly sliced

½ cup ketchup

2 tablespoons quick-cooking tapioca

*1 teaspoon liquid smoke
    (such as Colgin®)*

1 tablespoon cider vinegar

3 tablespoons light brown sugar

2 tablespoons kosher salt

*2 tablespoons GF Chili Powder
    (page 200)*

1 tablespoon ground black pepper

1 tablespoon onion powder

1 tablespoon garlic powder

1 tablespoon sweet or smoked paprika

1 teaspoon oregano

*½ teaspoon ground chipotle
    or more to taste*

*⅛ teaspoon ground cayenne
    or more to taste*

*5–6 pounds southern-style
    (country-style) pork ribs*

Barbecue Pork and Beans

Serves 8 (about 1 cup each)

Thick pieces of tender pork mingle with barbecue-sauced beans—what's not to love? These beans might not have the spiciness of New England–Style Baked Beans (see page 97), but they certainly do not lack flavor. Cook the beans overnight and assemble the recipe in the morning because, as in most baked bean recipes, the beans are cooked first and then cooked again in the sauce (see Technique Tip below).

*1 pound small white beans,
   rinsed and picked over*

1 onion, finely chopped

1½ cups ketchup

*½ cup water or vegetable broth
   (such as Pacific Natural Foods®)*

½ cup brown sugar

¼ cup cider vinegar or white vinegar

2 tablespoons Bragg Liquid Aminos®

*2 tablespoons real bacon bits
   (such as Hormel®)*

1 tablespoon minced garlic

*1½ teaspoons GF Chili Powder
   (see page 200)*

1 teaspoon paprika (sweet or smoked)

*¼ teaspoon cayenne pepper
   or more to taste*

*2 tablespoons GF Seasoning Salt
   (see page 199)*

3½–4 pounds pork shoulder

1. Add the beans to the slow cooker crock and cover them with at least 2 inches of water. Cover and cook 8 hours on LOW (or 4 hours on HIGH).

2. Drain the beans and add them back to the crock. Add the next 11 ingredients (onion through cayenne) to the crock and stir well.

3. Rub the GF Seasoning Salt all over the pork shoulder. Set the pork shoulder on top of the beans. Cover and cook 8–10 hours on LOW (or 5 hours on HIGH).

4. Transfer the pork to a platter and let it rest for about 10 minutes. When cool enough to handle, pull the pork off the bone and discard any visible fat. Shred the pork into large chunks and add it back to the crock. Stir gently to mix it into the beans.

TECHNIQUE TIP When preparing beans cooked in sweet or acidic liquids, the beans should be cooked beforehand or they will harden in the cooking liquid. After much trial and error, we found that cooking the beans overnight and then beginning the actual recipe the next morning works best.

Louisiana Red Beans and Rice

Serves 8 (about 1¼ cups bean mixture and ½ cup rice each)

This budget-friendly, hearty bean dish comes together very quickly and is perfectly suited to slow cooking. Louisiana Red Beans are typically served over rice. You can use leftover cooked rice or start preparing raw rice about half an hour before the beans are finished cooking. This recipe freezes well and reheats nicely.

1. Stir together all ingredients for the red beans except the Tabasco® in the slow cooker crock. Cover and cook 8–10 hours on LOW (or 4–5 hours on HIGH). Stir well before serving. The beans should be tender.

2. To prepare the rice: About 30 minutes before beans are done cooking, bring the water, butter, and salt to a boil in a medium saucepan over high heat. Add rice and stir well. Cover and reduce heat to medium/low. Cook for 20–25 minutes until water is absorbed and rice is tender.

3. To serve, divide rice between bowls and top each with about 1¼ cups of bean mixture. Offer Tabasco so people can season their beans.

Dairy-Free Variation

Replace butter with olive oil.

For the red beans

1 pound dry red kidney beans, picked over, soaked overnight or quick-soaked (see page 25 for soaking instructions)

1 pound andouille sausage (such as Wellshire™) or 1 pound kielbasa (such as Hillshire Farms®), cut into ½-inch slices

1 (32-ounce) package chicken broth (such as Pacific Natural Foods®)

½ cup water

1 onion, finely chopped

1 green or red bell pepper, finely chopped

2 bay leaves

1 tablespoon minced garlic

1¼ teaspoons poultry seasoning

1½ teaspoons Cajun seasoning (such as Luzianne®)

¼ teaspoon kosher salt

¼ teaspoon cayenne pepper or more to taste

Tabasco® to taste

For the rice

4 cups water

2 tablespoons butter

1 teaspoon kosher salt

2 cups long-grain white rice

Happy New Year Hoppin' John

Serves 6 (about 1⅓ cups each)

**Though nobody is quite sure how it got its name, the southern dish called Hoppin'
John is thought to ensure prosperity when served on New Year's Day. The peas
represent pennies, and serving this dish with cornbread (see page 188), to symbolize
gold, and collard or turnip greens, to represent paper money, is a tradition that we
find endearing. We think Hoppin' John is so tasty that it should be served more often
than once a year—and if it brings us any measure of financial success, all the better!**

5 cups chicken broth
   (such as Pacific Natural Foods®)

1 pound dry black-eyed peas,
   rinsed and picked over

1 green or red bell pepper, finely chopped

1 carrot, peeled and finely chopped
   (optional)

½ sweet onion, finely chopped

2 bay leaves

2 teaspoons minced garlic

1¼ teaspoons kosher salt or more to taste

¼ teaspoon ground black pepper or
   more to taste

¼ teaspoon dried thyme

¼ teaspoon crushed red pepper flakes

⅛ teaspoon ground allspice

1 smoked ham hock

2 cups cooked white or brown rice

Tabasco® (optional) to taste

1. Stir together the first 12 ingredients (broth through
allspice) in the slow cooker crock.

2. Nestle the ham hock in the center of the bean mixture.
Cover and cook 8 hours on LOW (or 4 hours on HIGH).

3. Remove the ham hock. Pull off any visible meat from the
hock and add it back to the pot (discard the bone and fat).
Stir in the rice and allow it heat through, about 15 minutes
uncovered.

Mimi's Classic Pork Roast and Vegetables with Gravy

Serves 6

This meal was always a favorite Sunday supper in Kimberly's house when she was growing up. Her mom made it about once a month, even in the summer—which reminds us to point out that slow cooking in the summer does not heat up the kitchen as the oven does and is convenient when you're playing outside since you don't have to go tend to dinner.

1. Spray the inside of the slow cooker crock with cooking spray. Add the potatoes and shallots to the slow cooker crock in an even layer. Add the chicken broth and Bragg Liquid Aminos; set aside.

2. In a separate bowl, whisk together the next 8 ingredients (oil through paprika). Coat the pork loin with this mixture and place it on top of the potatoes. Arrange the carrots around the pork loin. Cover and cook 8 hours on LOW (or 4 hours on HIGH).

3. Transfer the pork to a plate. Use a slotted spoon to transfer the vegetables to a serving platter and tent both roast and vegetables with foil; let rest 10 minutes before slicing meat.

4. Strain the cooking juices through a fine mesh sieve into a saucepan (you should have about 2 cups). Place the saucepan over medium-high heat. In a separate bowl, whisk together the water, cornstarch, and Gravy Master. Add the cornstarch mixture to the cooking juices and stir until gravy comes to a full boil. Once the mixture thickens, remove from heat.

5. Slice the roast, arrange the pork and vegetables on a platter family-style, and offer the gravy alongside.

Nonstick cooking spray

2-pound bag mini gourmet potatoes (Yukon Gold, fingerling, or Red Bliss)

4 shallots, thinly sliced

1 cup chicken broth (such as Pacific Natural Foods®)

1 tablespoon Bragg Liquid Aminos®

2 tablespoons olive oil

1 tablespoon minced garlic

1 tablespoon dried rosemary

2 teaspoons Dijon mustard

¾ teaspoon dried thyme

1 teaspoon kosher salt

½ teaspoon ground black pepper

¼ teaspoon paprika

1 (2½-pound) boneless pork loin roast

1 pound carrots, peeled, halved, and cut into 3-inch lengths

3 tablespoons water

2 tablespoons cornstarch

1 teaspoon Gravy Master®

Dijon Pork Roast with Brandied Mushroom Sauce

Serves 6

2 tablespoons quick-cooking tapioca

1 leek, halved lengthwise, washed well, and thinly sliced

2 tablespoons butter

1 teaspoon minced garlic

1½ pounds sliced white mushrooms

½ teaspoon kosher salt

¼ teaspoon ground black pepper

3 tablespoons good-quality brandy

1 (2½ pound) boneless pork loin roast

2 tablespoons Dijon mustard (such as Grey Poupon®)

1 tablespoon olive oil

½ teaspoon GF Seasoning Salt (see page 199)

½ teaspoon dried thyme

¼ teaspoon dried rosemary

¼ teaspoon dried oregano

2 tablespoons heavy cream

finely chopped parsley (optional) for garnish

Pork roast is one of our slow cooking mainstays. It is so versatile and always delivers a flavorful feast (and equally delicious leftovers). In this recipe, the roast is rubbed with a mixture of Dijon mustard and dried herbs. The sauce is made from mushrooms and leeks with just a hint of brandy and cream. Serve this dish with rice and a steamed green vegetable like asparagus.

1. Sprinkle the tapioca and leeks into the slow cooker crock; set aside.

2. Warm the butter in a large nonstick skillet over medium heat. When hot, add the garlic, mushrooms, salt, and pepper. Cook and stir mushrooms for about 10 minutes (they will give off a lot of liquid and brown up nicely). Add the brandy and cook about 2 minutes. Transfer the mushroom mixture to the crock in an even layer. Do not stir.

3. Place the pork into the crock on top of the mushrooms.

4. In a separate bowl, whisk together the mustard, olive oil, seasoning salt, thyme, rosemary, and oregano. Use a pastry brush or the back of a spoon to coat the top and sides of the pork with the mustard mixture. Cover and cook 8 hours on LOW (or 4 hours on HIGH).

5. Transfer the pork to a plate. Scrape away any mushrooms from the bottom of the pork and return them to the crock. Tent the roast with foil and let it rest 10 minutes before slicing.

6. Stir the cream into the mushrooms and sauce. To serve, spoon the sauce over top of the sliced pork. Garnish with parsley, if desired.

Dairy-Free Variation

Replace butter with olive oil.
Omit the cream.

TECHNIQUE TIP Keeping kitchen knives sharp is important for a couple of reasons. First, it makes the work easier and neater. For example, part of the pork tenderloin is covered with a tough, pearly membrane called the silverskin, which should be trimmed off before cooking. The sharper your knife, the neater the trim job will be (and the less waste you'll have). Secondly, sharp knives are actually safer than dull ones. Sharp knives slice through things easily, so you don't need to put much pressure on the knife in order to make it cut. Pushing a dull knife through food, on the other hand, can result in slippage and cuts. Whether you sharpen your own knives or take them to a cookware or knife store to have the job done, it's a good idea to keep your knives sharp all the time.

Rosemary, Garlic, and Lemon Pork Roast

Serves 6

This boneless pork roast is infused with the complementary flavors of rosemary, garlic, and lemon. Along with potatoes—and the quick addition of fresh spinach—this dish is a satisfying, complete meal.

*2 tablespoons fresh rosemary leaves
     or 1 tablespoon dried rosemary leaves*

1 tablespoon minced garlic

¾ teaspoon kosher salt or more to taste

½ teaspoon ground black pepper

1 (2½–pound) boneless pork loin roast

1 teaspoon quick-cooking tapioca

1 shallot, thinly sliced

*3 large, round, white or Yukon Gold
     potatoes, quartered lengthwise*

2 tablespoons butter, cut into small cubes

½ cup dry white wine

1 lemon, washed and sliced

1 (5-ounce) package fresh baby spinach

1. Stir together the rosemary, garlic, salt, and pepper in a small bowl. Rub the spice mixture all over the pork roast; set aside.

2. Sprinkle the tapioca into the slow cooker crock. Add the shallot and potatoes to the crock. Sprinkle the butter cubes over the potatoes and add the wine. Place the pork roast on top of potatoes. Arrange the lemon slices over the pork and potatoes. Cover and cook 8 hours on LOW (or 4 hours on HIGH).

3. Using tongs, transfer lemon slices to a small bowl. Using a fork, gently press the juice out of the lemons and add the juice back to the crock (discard the lemon slices). Transfer the pork to a cutting board, tent with foil, and let it rest for at least 10 minutes before slicing. Using a slotted spoon, scoop the potatoes into a bowl. Stir the spinach into the remaining cooking juices until wilted.

4. Slice the pork against the grain. To serve, place a few potato pieces onto each plate, arrange pork slices next to the potatoes, and spoon spinach and sauce over the potatoes and pork.

Dairy-Free Variation

Replace butter with olive oil.

Apple Cranberry Pork Roast

Serves 6

Easy and delicious, this meal is slow cooking at its finest. The well-seasoned pork is served alongside a generous portion of sweet, spiced apples. The cranberries offer a punch of color and flavor to complete the dish. Serve with rice and a steamed green vegetable.

1. Stir together the sauce ingredients in the slow cooker crock; set aside.

2. Stir the butter and seasonings together in a small bowl. Coat the pork with the seasonings. Place pork into the slow cooker, fat side up. Cover and cook 8 hours on LOW (or 4 hours on HIGH).

3. Transfer the pork to a cutting board, tent with foil, and let it rest for at least 10 minutes before slicing. Stir the sauce and serve it alongside the sliced pork.

Dairy-Free Variation

Replace butter with olive oil.

For the sauce

4 apples (such as Golden Delicious, Braeburn, or Cameo), peeled and chopped

1¼ cups fresh cranberries

⅓ cup sugar

¼ cup ginger ale (regular, not diet)

2 tablespoons cornstarch

½ teaspoon balsamic vinegar

⅛ teaspoon ground ginger

⅛ teaspoon ground nutmeg or cloves (optional)

⅛ teaspoon kosher salt

For the pork

2 tablespoons melted butter

2 teaspoons poultry seasoning

¼ teaspoon onion powder

¼ teaspoon kosher salt

¼ teaspoon ground black pepper

1 (2½-pound) boneless pork loin

Pork Tenderloin Medallions with Pomegranate-Cherry Sauce

Serves 3

This savory-sweet treatment is a little more special than everyday fare, so it's perfect for Valentine's Day or any time you want something nice, but easy. Note that this recipe only takes four hours to cook (pork tenderloin is a very quick-cooking cut of meat), so plan accordingly. Round out the meal with mashed potatoes and your favorite green vegetable.

½ cup chicken broth
(such as Pacific Natural Foods®)

½ cup bottled pomegranate-cherry juice

2 tablespoons cornstarch

2 tablespoons red wine (optional)

¾ cup dried cherries, divided

½ small onion, finely chopped

1 teaspoon kosher salt

½ teaspoon garlic powder

½ teaspoon Italian seasoning

¼ teaspoon ground black pepper

pinch cayenne pepper

1 (16-ounce) all natural pork
tenderloin, trimmed

1 cup cherry preserves

1. Whisk together the broth, juice, cornstarch, and wine (if using) in the slow cooker crock. Sprinkle in ¼ cup of the cherries (reserve remainder for finishing sauce) and the onion; set aside.

2. In a gallon-sized zip-top plastic bag, combine all the seasonings (salt through cayenne). Add the pork to the bag, seal it, and shake to coat the pork with the seasoning mixture. Add the pork to the slow cooker, along with any seasonings remaining in the bag. Do not stir; let the pork sit on top of the broth, cherries, and onion.

3. Cover and cook 4 hours on LOW (HIGH heat is not recommended). Transfer the cooked tenderloin to a plate; tent with foil and let rest while finishing sauce.

4. Add the preserves and remaining ½ cup dried cherries to the crock and stir well to make the sauce. Cover and let sauce heat while finishing the pork.

5. On a clean cutting board, cut the cooked tenderloin, on a diagonal, into ¾-inch thick medallions. Transfer the medallions to the crock and stir to coat them with sauce and rewarm them. To serve, use tongs to remove medallions from the crock; divide them between plates and ladle the sauce over each portion.

DAIRY-FREE

12
Beef

Recipe Variation

DAIRY-FREE

Beef with Lentils and Mushrooms

Serves 6 (about 1⅓ cups each)

In this recipe, tender cubes of beef, baby bella mushrooms, and nutritious, rosemary-seasoned lentils make a hearty supper dish. Be aware that raw mushrooms should be precooked for slow cooking to ensure optimal flavor and texture. Make it easy on yourself—get the mushrooms cooking on the stove while you prep the rest of the ingredients.

2 tablespoons butter

2 (8-ounce) packages sliced
   baby bella mushrooms

½ pound lentils (1 generous cup),
   rinsed and picked over

3 shallots, thinly sliced

2 carrots, halved lengthwise
   and cut into ¼-inch slices

2 pounds lean stew beef,
   cut into 1-inch chunks

1 bay leaf

2 teaspoons beef bouillon (such as
   Organic Better than Bouillon®)

2 teaspoons minced garlic

½ teaspoon celery salt

½ teaspoon ground black pepper

½ teaspoon dried rosemary

½ cup dry red or white wine

2 cups water

¾ cup crumbled feta cheese

¼ cup finely chopped flat leaf parsley

1. Add butter to a large nonstick skillet over medium heat. When hot, add the mushrooms. Cook and stir mushrooms for about 10 minutes (they will give off a lot of liquid and brown up nicely). Turn off heat.

2. Place the lentils into the slow cooker crock, spreading to make an even bottom layer. Top with a layer of shallots, then the carrots, and then the beef. Place the bay leaf on top.

3. Add the bouillon, garlic, celery salt, black pepper, rosemary, wine, and water to the crock. Top everything with an even layer of the cooked mushrooms. Do not stir. Cover and cook 8 hours on LOW (or 4 hours on HIGH).

4. Before serving, stir well. Garnish each portion with 2 tablespoons feta and 2 teaspoons parsley.

Dairy-Free Variation

Replace butter with olive oil.
Omit feta.

Chuck Wagon Cowboy Beans

DAIRY-FREE

Serves 6 generously (about 1⅔ cups each)

The secret ingredient in Cowboy Beans is coffee. Given the "waste not, want not" credo of living on the range, cowboys would pour any leftover coffee into the bean pot. We've embellished our Cowboy Beans with a big ol' pot roast. This recipe makes for great Super Bowl fare, especially if the Dallas Cowboys are playing. Like other baked beans, the pinto beans must be cooked before they are baked in their sweet and spicy sauce, making this a two-day recipe. For ease, we like to precook the beans overnight and assemble this recipe the next morning.

1. Add the beans to the slow cooker crock and cover them with at least 2 inches of water. Cover and cook 8 hours on LOW (or 4 hours on HIGH).

2. Drain the beans and add them back to the crock. Stir in 1 can of the chilies and the next 11 ingredients (onion through chili powder) to the crock.

3. In a separate bowl, stir together the remaining can of chilies, the seasoning salt, and Gravy Master. Pat the mixture over the pot roast and set it on top of the beans. Scrape any remaining seasoning mixture onto the top of the pot roast. Cover and cook 9–10 hours on LOW (or 4–5 hours on HIGH).

4. Transfer the pot roast to a platter and let it rest for about 10 minutes. Skim and discard any visible fat from the beans. When the pot roast is cool enough to handle, cut it into large chunks and add them back to the crock. Stir gently to mix the meat and beans together.

5. Garnish portions with scallions and offer Tabasco, if desired.

1 pound pinto beans, rinsed and picked over

2 (4.5-ounce) cans chopped green chilies, divided

1 onion, finely chopped

1 jalapeño, seeded and finely chopped

2 tablespoons real bacon bits (such Hormel®)

1 cup ketchup

⅓ cup brown sugar

2 tablespoons brown mustard (such as Gulden's®)

2 tablespoons tomato paste

1 tablespoon instant coffee

1 tablespoon cider vinegar

1 tablespoon minced garlic

1 tablespoon GF Chili Powder (see page 200)

1 tablespoon GF Seasoning Salt (see page 199)

1 tablespoon Gravy Master®

1 4–pound beef chuck pot roast, fat trimmed

chopped scallions (optional) for garnish

Tabasco® (optional) to taste

Beef Stroganoff

Serves 4 (about 1¼ cups each)

Beef Stroganoff is usually considered a dish of the 1950s in America, but in truth it appeared in U.S. cookbooks as early as the 1930s. It's the kind of family-friendly comfort food that most of us find irresistible during the winter months. This recipe contains all the standard ingredients you're accustomed to; it's just easier since it's slow cooked! Serve it over your favorite gluten-free pasta or rice.

1¼ pounds sirloin tip steak, trimmed of visible fat and cut into ½-inch slices

1 medium onion, chopped

1 (8-ounce) package sliced baby bella mushrooms

¼ cup cold water

2 tablespoons cornstarch

1 tablespoon beef bouillon (such as Organic Better than Bouillon®)

1 teaspoon kosher salt

1 teaspoon minced garlic

½ cup sour cream

2 tablespoons chopped fresh dill (optional)

1. Add the steak, onions, and mushrooms to the slow cooker crock; set aside.

2. In a small bowl, stir together the water and cornstarch until starch is dissolved and mixture has no lumps. Pour it into the slow cooker crock; then stir in the beef bouillon, salt, and garlic. Cover and cook on LOW 8 hours (or 4 hours on HIGH).

3. Turn off the slow cooker; stir in the sour cream.

4. To serve, spoon the Stroganoff over noodles or rice. Garnish each portion with fresh dill, if desired.

Pepper and Onion Swiss Steak

Serves 4 (one steak and about 1 cup vegetables each)

This is the kind of retro dish that people remember eating as kids, only our version is easier than the original—though just as tasty. It makes use of an inexpensive cut of meat and is nicely seasoned with lots of peppers and onions in a light tomato sauce. Kimberly's Dad likes this recipe best when served over steamed, long-grain, white rice.

1. Sprinkle tapioca over the bottom of the slow cooker crock; set aside.

2. Stir together the next 11 ingredients (onion through black pepper) in a bowl. Transfer the mixture to the slow cooker crock, spreading it in an even layer; do not stir. Cover and cook 8 hours on LOW (4 hours on HIGH).

3. Stir well before serving. Garnish each bowl with parsley, if desired.

3 tablespoons quick-cooking tapioca

1 sweet onion, thinly sliced

3 sweet bell peppers (red, green, or a mixture), sliced

4 cube steaks (about 1½ pounds total)

1 (8-ounce) can tomato sauce

1 tablespoon tomato paste

1 tablespoon olive oil

2 teaspoons beef bouillon (such as Organic Better than Bouillon®)

1½ teaspoons minced garlic

1 teaspoon Italian seasoning

½ teaspoon kosher salt

¼ teaspoon ground black pepper

2 tablespoons finely chopped fresh parsley (optional)

Swiss Steak with Creamy Mushrooms and Vegetables

Serves 4 (1 steak and about 1 cup of vegetables each)

Cooking with canned creamed soup is out of the question if you're following a gluten-free diet. This creamy Swiss steak uses basic cream cheese to achieve its luxurious texture.

2 tablespoons olive oil

1 pound sliced white mushrooms

1½ teaspoons minced garlic

1 pound bag frozen mixed vegetables, thawed

1 onion, finely chopped

1½ teaspoons Italian seasoning

¾ teaspoon kosher salt

½ teaspoon ground black pepper

¼ teaspoon paprika

4 cube steaks (about 1½ pounds total)

¼ cup grated Parmesan cheese

4 ounces cream cheese (regular or light)

finely chopped fresh parsley or basil (optional)

1. Add oil to a large nonstick skillet over medium heat. When hot, add the mushrooms and garlic. Cook and stir mushrooms for about 10 minutes (they will give off a lot of liquid and brown up nicely). Turn off heat.

2. In a separate bowl, stir together the vegetables, onion, Italian seasoning, salt, black pepper, and paprika. Add the mushrooms and stir to combine. Pour ⅓ of this mixture into the crock. Top with the steaks. Pour remaining vegetables over the steaks; do not stir. Cover and cook 8 hours on LOW (or 4 hours on HIGH).

3. Remove the steaks with tongs and set aside (cover with foil to keep warm). Add Parmesan and cream cheese to the crock and stir until cheese is melted and mixture is well combined.

4. To serve, place one steak on each plate and spoon about 1 cup of vegetable mixture on top. Garnish each plate with fresh parsley, if desired.

INGREDIENT INFO Cube steaks are typically beef round steaks that have been mechanically tenderized. Cube steaks are often used to make the classic Southern comfort food—chicken-fried steak. A true budget cut of beef, round steaks are very lean and benefit from a generous coating of well-seasoned sauce.

Texas Barbecue Brisket

Serves 8–12, depending on appetites

If any cut of meat was created for slow cooking, it is beef brisket, a tough cut of meat that becomes very tender after a long, slow cook. Texans have a pretty fabulous way with brisket and this recipe was created in their honor. Don't let the large amount of seasonings scare you away! A five-pound brisket is a big piece of beef and requires ample seasoning. A six-quart slow cooker is best for this recipe.

1. Stir the first 9 ingredients (salt through cayenne) together in a large bowl. Rub the spice mixture all over the brisket and set aside.

2. Stir together the onion, ketchup, and liquid smoke in the slow cooker crock. Place the brisket on top. Sprinkle any remaining spice mixture (from the bowl) over the top of the brisket. Cover and cook 9–10 hours on LOW (or 4–5 hours on HIGH).

3. Transfer the brisket to a platter and cover with foil. Allow the brisket to rest for at least 10 minutes before cutting it into thin slices, against the grain.

4. While the meat rests, give the onion mixture a good stir. Skim any visible fat from the surface and discard. Pour the cooking liquid and onion over the meat slices and serve.

3 tablespoons kosher salt

3 tablespoons GF Chili Powder (see page 200)

1 tablespoon ground black pepper

1 tablespoon garlic powder

1 tablespoon light brown sugar

2 teaspoons onion powder

1 teaspoon dried oregano

1 teaspoon ground chipotle pepper

½–1 teaspoon ground cayenne pepper, to taste

1 (5-pound) beef brisket, trimmed of visible fat

1 sweet onion, thinly sliced

⅓ cup ketchup

½ teaspoon liquid smoke (such as Colgin®)

DAIRY-FREE

Old-School Stuffed Peppers

Serves 6 (1 pepper each)

We think these stuffed peppers are just as great-tasting as Mama used to make—only easier. Before you start, make sure that your slow cooker is large enough to hold six bell peppers; we needed a 6-quart cooker. These peppers are practically a complete meal—veggies, protein, and grain. Just add a nice green salad or some fresh fruit and call it done.

6 medium-sized sweet bell peppers
   (2 each of red, green, and yellow
   are nice)

1 pound ground "meatloaf" mix
   (ground beef, pork, and veal)

3 cups prepared pasta sauce or marinara
   (such as Muir Glen®), divided

½ cup uncooked brown rice

¼ cup shredded Parmesan cheese

1 egg

1 tablespoon tamari (such as San-J®)

1 teaspoon minced garlic

½ teaspoon Italian seasoning

½ teaspoon kosher salt

¼ teaspoon garlic powder

¼ teaspoon GF Chili Powder
   (see page 200)

¾ cup shredded, part-skim
   mozzarella cheese

1. Cut the tops off the peppers, remove stems, and save tops for another use. Remove the seeds and ribs from the inside of the peppers. Set peppers aside.

2. Use your hands to mix together the meatloaf mix, 1 cup of the pasta sauce, and the next 9 ingredients (rice through chili powder) in a medium mixing bowl until well combined. Stuff the meat mixture into the peppers.

3. Pour 1 cup of the pasta sauce into the bottom of the slow cooker crock; then place the stuffed peppers inside the crock, standing them upright. Cover and cook 6 hours on LOW (3 hours on HIGH).

4. Remove the lid and top each pepper with 2 tablespoons of the mozzarella. Turn off the slow cooker, cover, and let the peppers rest for 5 minutes, until cheese is melted. Use a serving spoon to transfer the peppers to a platter. Stir the remaining 1 cup of pasta sauce into the sauce in the crock. To serve, ladle the sauce onto individual plates, dividing it evenly. Top each sauce portion with a stuffed pepper.

Classic Pot Roast with Potatoes

Serves 6

Well suited to slow cooking, beef pot roast is a favorite Sunday supper with us. This recipe is a complete meal with potatoes and carrots, but feel free to add a salad— Mixed Greens with Dates, Pine Nuts, and Gorgonzola (see page 194) would be perfect.

1. Layer the potatoes, shallots, and tomatoes in the slow cooker crock. Top with the bay leaf and then the pot roast. Arrange carrots around the meat.

2. In a separate bowl, whisk together the next 8 ingredients (tomato paste through black pepper). Spread this mixture over the pot roast. Cover and cook 9–10 hours on LOW (or 4–5 hours on HIGH).

3. Transfer the pot roast to a platter and cover with foil for at least 10 minutes before slicing. Use a slotted spoon to transfer the vegetables to a serving bowl. Skim and discard any visible fat from the surface of the sauce and stir sauce well.

4. Slice the pot roast against the grain and arrange slices on the serving platter. Spoon the sauce over the beef slices. Garnish with parsley, if desired.

1 (2-pound) bag mini gourmet potatoes (such as Yukon Gold or fingerling)

3 shallots, thinly sliced (or 1 small onion)

1 (14.5-ounce) can petite diced tomatoes, drained

1 bay leaf

4 pounds boneless chuck beef pot roast

1 pound carrots, peeled and cut into 3-inch lengths

2 tablespoons tomato paste

2 tablespoons dry red wine

1 tablespoon Gravy Master®

2 teaspoons dried rosemary (or 1 tablespoon fresh rosemary leaves)

2 teaspoons minced garlic

1 teaspoon poultry seasoning

1½ teaspoons kosher salt

½ teaspoon ground black pepper

finely chopped parsley (optional) for garnish

Bolognese Pot Roast

Serves 8

This Italian-inspired pot roast is a great change of pace from the typical Sunday pot roast! The sauce can be served "rustic," with chunky veggies, or you can puree it for a smoother, more "refined" sauce. Either way, we recommend serving it with your favorite gluten-free pasta or Slow-Cooked Polenta (see page 102) for a complete meal.

3 celery stalks, finely chopped

2 carrots, peeled and finely chopped

1 onion, finely chopped

¼ cup tomato paste

2 tablespoons real bacon bits
   (such as Hormel®)

2 tablespoons quick-cooking tapioca

4 pounds boneless chuck beef pot roast

1 (28-ounce) can whole tomatoes

2 teaspoons balsamic vinegar

2 teaspoon minced garlic

1 ½ teaspoons oregano

1 teaspoon kosher salt

¾ teaspoon dried thyme

½ teaspoon ground black pepper

¼ teaspoon crushed red pepper

⅛ teaspoon ground nutmeg

2 tablespoons heavy cream

finely chopped fresh basil or fresh parsley
   (optional) for garnish

1. Stir together the first 6 ingredients (celery through tapioca) in the slow cooker crock. Place the pot roast on top of the vegetables; set aside.

2. In a separate bowl, stir together the next 9 ingredients (tomatoes through nutmeg); pour this mixture over the roast. Cover and cook 9–10 hours on LOW (or 4–5 hours on HIGH). Transfer the pot roast to a platter and cover with foil. Allow the pot roast to rest for at least 10 minutes before cutting it into thin slices, against the grain.

3. Stir the cream into the vegetables. If you prefer a chunky sauce, you're done! To make a smooth sauce, puree the vegetables with an immersion blender. Alternatively, you can puree the vegetables in a food processor or blender (but be careful because the sauce will be very hot).

4. Serve each portion of meat with about 1 cup of vegetables or sauce. Garnish with basil, if desired.

Dairy-Free Variation

Omit the heavy cream.

Steak Diane Pot Roast with Mushrooms and Potatoes

Serves 6

DAIRY-FREE

Taking its cue from the signature flavors of Steak Diane, this pot roast is accented with garlic, shallots, and brandy. Serve it with steamed green beans for a complete dinner. Leftovers? No worries—pot roast reheats beautifully in the oven or microwave.

1. Sprinkle tapioca in the bottom of the slow cooker crock. Layer the vegetables in the crock, starting with the potatoes and ending with the shallots. Place the roast on top of the vegetables.

2. Whisk together the brandy, garlic, mustard, bouillon, salt, and pepper in a small mixing bowl until smooth. Pour the mixture over the pot roast. Cover and cook 9–10 hours on LOW (or 4–5 hours on HIGH).

3. Transfer roast to a cutting board. Stir the sauce and vegetables and skim any visible fat. Slice the roast against the grain. Divide vegetables between plates; top with meat slices and sauce.

1 tablespoon quick-cooking tapioca

2 pounds small red potatoes, washed and halved

16 ounces sliced white mushrooms

4 shallots, finely chopped

3 pounds pot roast, visible exterior fat trimmed

½ cup good-quality brandy

2 tablespoons minced garlic

2 tablespoons Dijon mustard (such as Grey Poupon®)

2 teaspoons beef bouillon (such as Organic Better than Bouillon®)

½ teaspoon kosher salt

½ teaspoon ground black pepper

13

Cook Once, Eat Twice Recipes

Making good use of leftovers makes sense economically and also saves time. In this chapter we've included some of our favorite recipes that reuse a slow-cooked item or entrée. For example, cooking Chili and Lime Brisket (see page 163) one night for dinner and setting aside some of the meat means that Beef Tacos with Black Bean and Corn Salsa (see page 164) can be on the menu the following day.

Recipe *Variation*
DAIRY-FREE

Roasted Garlic

Makes about ¾ cup

Roasted garlic is a snap to make in a slow cooker, and such a handy ingredient to have on hand. Kimberly likes to make an easy cracker spread for her husband, Mark, by adding the roasted garlic to whipped chive cream cheese (see recipe on page 157). Roasted garlic can also be stirred into beans, mashed potatoes, soup, and pasta sauce (see recipe on page 158) and used to season salad dressings. Unlike its raw counterpart, roasted garlic is smooth and almost sweet. Do not skip the aluminum foil step—we did and found that the recipe did not work as well nor taste as good as the wrapped bulbs.

6 whole bulbs garlic
4 teaspoons olive oil
¼ teaspoon kosher salt
⅛ teaspoon ground black pepper
fresh rosemary or thyme sprig (optional)

1. Cut a thin slice off the top of each bulb, just enough to expose the very tops of a few cloves.

2. Tear a piece of aluminum foil big enough to wrap all the bulbs together. Place the bulbs on the foil, cut side up. Drizzle the bulbs with the olive oil, sprinkle them with salt and pepper, and top them with a fresh herb sprig, if desired. Pull the foil over the top of the bulbs and seal the foil, making a packet.

3. Place the packet into the slow cooker. Cover and cook 4–5 hours on LOW (or 2–2½ hours on HIGH).

4. Let the garlic bulbs cool, uncovered, in the slow cooker. Once the bulbs are cool enough to handle, squeeze the softened garlic cloves into a bowl. Most of the garlic will come out easily; you may have to trim the tops of some cloves that remained intact during cooking. Mash the garlic with a fork. Roasted garlic can be refrigerated or frozen until needed.

Mark's Three-Ingredient Cracker Spread

Serves 10 (about 2 tablespoons each)

This cracker spread is so easy to make and much better than store-bought spreads. It is also fantastic for gluten-free tortilla wraps with turkey and lettuce.

Mix all the ingredients together in a small bowl. Serve with your favorite gluten-free crackers. This spread is especially good with Mary's Gone Crackers® Black Pepper Crackers.

1 (8-ounce) container whipped, chive cream cheese

¼ cup mashed Roasted Garlic (see page 156)

2–3 dashes of Tabasco®

Brown Rice Fusilli with Roasted Garlic Marinara

Serves 8 (about 1¼ cups each)

When people are eating gluten-free, pasta is one of the dishes they tend to miss the most. Fortunately, food manufacturers are responding by producing more varieties of good-quality gluten-free pastas. For example, rice fusilli (also known as rotini) pairs well with this chunky, homemade marinara—it's guaranteed to quell your pasta cravings. Don't be afraid of the amount of garlic in this recipe—precooking and roasting keeps it mild.

For the sauce

3 tablespoons good-quality olive oil

1 onion, finely chopped

1 teaspoon minced garlic

¾ teaspoon kosher salt, more to taste

¼ teaspoon crushed red pepper

1 (28-ounce) can Italian peeled tomatoes, coarsely chopped or crushed by hand

2 tablespoons mashed Roasted Garlic (see page 156)

1¼ teaspoons dried oregano

1 pound brown rice fusilli (such as Trader Joe's®)

grated Parmesan (optional)

1. Warm the oil in a medium saucepan over medium heat. When hot, add the onion, minced garlic, salt, and red pepper; cook and stir until onion begins to soften, about 5 minutes. Add tomatoes, mashed garlic, and oregano and bring to a simmer. Reduce heat to medium-low. Partially cover and cook for 20 minutes, stirring occasionally.

2. While the sauce cooks, prepare the fusilli according to package instructions. Drain the pasta; do not rinse it.

3. To serve, toss the pasta and sauce together in a large bowl. Serve with Parmesan, if desired.

Dairy-Free Variation

Omit the Parmesan.

Corned Beef and Cabbage Boiled Dinner

Serves 6

We feel the traditional St. Patty's Day meal should be enjoyed year-round because it is so easy to make. This recipe produces just the right amount of vegetables for one meal and enough leftover corned beef to make Corned Beef Hash (see page 160) a day or two later. This recipe must be made in a six-quart slow cooker. If you own a smaller slow cooker, boil the potatoes on the stove-top instead of slow cooking them.

1. Layer the first 10 ingredients in the slow cooker crock, starting with the potatoes on the bottom and ending with the allspice. Place the brisket on top of the vegetables, cutting it in half if necessary to fit into your crock.

2. Add enough water to come halfway up the corned beef. (The amount of liquid will actually increase as the vegetables and corned beef cook.) Cover and cook 9–10 hours on LOW (or 4–5 hours on HIGH).

3. Transfer the corned beef to a platter and cover with foil. Allow the meat to rest for at least 10 minutes before cutting it into thin slices, against the grain. Use a slotted spoon to transfer the vegetables to a serving platter. Spoon some cooking juices over the corned beef slices and sprinkle parsley over all, if desired.

Dairy-Free Variation

Omit the butter.

2 pounds Red Bliss potatoes
   (or other small, red potatoes)

1 pound carrots, peeled and cut into
   3-inch lengths

¼ pound pearl onions, peeled
   (or frozen pearl onions, thawed)

½ head cabbage (about 1 ½ pounds),
   cored and cut into 1-inch slices

½ teaspoon ground black pepper

¼ teaspoon kosher salt

2 tablespoons butter

1 tablespoon cider vinegar

1 bay leaf

pinch ground allspice

4 pounds corned beef brisket,
   visible fat trimmed

finely chopped parsley (optional)
   for garnish

Corned Beef Hash

Serves 6 (about 1 cup each)

In Kimberly's opinion, the best reason to make the Corned Beef and Cabbage Boiled Dinner (see page 159) is to have corned beef hash the next day, for the ultimate breakfast. This recipe is the one we like best, but feel free to embellish it with other veggies and seasonings to give it your personal touch. Serve it with poached or fried eggs and gluten-free toast.

2 tablespoons butter, divided

½ onion, finely chopped

3 cups finely chopped, cooked corned beef (from Corned Beef and Cabbage Boiled Dinner, page 159)

3 cups cooked potatoes, finely chopped

¼ teaspoon ground black pepper or more to taste

kosher salt to taste, if needed

1. Melt 1 tablespoon of the butter in a large nonstick skillet over medium-high heat. When hot, add the onion and cook and stir until softened, about 5 minutes.

2. While the onion cooks, stir together the corned beef, potatoes, and pepper in a large mixing bowl. Add the cooked onion to the mixture and stir well to combine.

3. Melt the remaining tablespoon of butter in the large skillet. When hot, add the corned beef mixture to the skillet and use the back of a spatula to firmly press the mixture into the pan. Let the hash cook for 10 minutes without stirring until golden and crispy on the bottom. Continue to cook, stirring occasionally, for about 8 more minutes, until heated through and lightly browned.

Dairy-Free Variation

Replace butter with olive oil.

TECHNIQUE TIP You can make quick work of chopping the corned beef, potatoes, and onions by using a food processor or electric chopper, but we recommend that you process each ingredient separately so that you achieve the right consistency.

Easiest Pulled Pork

Serves 10 (about ¾ cup each)

Pulled pork—tender pork that is shredded by hand—is typically associated with the southern United States, where local preferences dictate recipe variations. Our version is sufficiently smoky for our taste, but feel free to increase the seasonings, if you like. Gluten-free rolls stuffed with pulled pork make a great half-time snack or casual party fare. You could also use the pork in Pork and Bean Tortilla Casserole (page 162), in tacos, or served on its own with mashed potatoes. Leftovers can be frozen for later use. Easy, versatile, delish—this recipe will become a favorite.

1. Stir together the GF Barbecue Seasoning, paprika, and salt in a small bowl. Rub the mixture all over the pork, using all the seasoning mixture.

2. Place the roast in the slow cooker crock and top with the onion slices. Cover and cook on LOW for 8 hours. Let the roast rest, covered, for 10 minutes.

3. Lift the roast out of the slow cooker (leave the cooking juices in the crock) and transfer to a cutting board. Shred the pork, using two forks.

4. Skim the fat off the surface of the cooking juices and stir in the liquid smoke. Put the pork back into the crock to absorb some of the cooking juices. Serve the pork directly from the crock, or transfer it to a serving dish.

2 tablespoons GF Barbecue Seasoning (page 201)

2 teaspoons smoked paprika

1 teaspoon kosher salt

1 (3-pound) boneless pork loin roast

1 small onion, thinly sliced

½ teaspoon liquid smoke (such as Colgin®)

Pork and Bean Tortilla Casserole

Serves 10

With leftovers from our Easiest Pulled Pork (see page 161), this Tex-Mex casserole comes together in about 20 minutes. We like the addition of sautéed zucchini to amp up the vegetable quotient. This casserole is perfect on its own, or you can add a simple salad.

Nonstick cooking spray

1 tablespoon canola oil

*3 small zucchini,
    chopped into ½-inch pieces*

½ onion, finely chopped

1 teaspoon minced garlic

¼ teaspoon ground black pepper

*8 cups restaurant-style tortilla chips
    (such as Tostitos®)*

3 cups Easiest Pulled Pork (see page 161)

1 (15-ounce) container ricotta cheese

*2 cups Mexican blend shredded cheese,
    divided*

*1 (15.5-ounce) can pinto beans,
    rinsed and drained*

*1 (16-ounce) jar salsa
    (such as Muir Glen®)*

sour cream (optional) for garnish

avocado, chopped (optional) for garnish

1. Preheat the oven to 350°F. Grease a 13 x 9-inch baking pan with cooking spray; set aside.

2. Heat oil in a large nonstick skillet over medium heat. When hot, add zucchini, onion, garlic, and black pepper. Cook and stir until zucchini is tender and lightly browned, about 10 minutes.

3. While the zucchini cooks, make a layer of chips in the baking pan. (It does not have to be a perfectly even layer.) Spread the pork over the chips in the pan.

4. Drop ricotta by spoonfuls on top of the pork. Sprinkle 1 cup of the shredded cheese over the pork. Add another layer of chips, gently pressing down to flatten the ricotta slightly.

5. Add the pinto beans to the cooked zucchini and toss well. Spread the bean mixture over the chips in the baking pan, and then top with a final layer of chips.

6. Spoon the salsa over the top and sprinkle with the remaining cheese. Coat a sheet of aluminum foil with cooking spray and use it to cover the casserole, greased-side down. Bake casserole for 30 minutes.

7. Remove foil and bake an additional 10 minutes. The cheese will brown slightly and the casserole will be bubbling. Let the casserole rest 10 minutes before cutting into 10 pieces for serving. Garnish casserole with sour cream and/or avocado, if desired.

Chili and Lime Brisket

Serves 8–12, depending on appetites

We are big fans of slow-cooked brisket because we love all the possibilities for using the leftovers. This particular brisket can be used to fill tacos (see page 164), make a corn tortilla casserole, or top a salad. Adjust the heat and spiciness to suit your taste by increasing or decreasing the number of jalapeños and amount of cayenne pepper in the recipe.

1. Stir together 1 can of the green chilies and the next 4 ingredients (onion through tapioca) in the slow cooker crock.

2. In a separate bowl, stir together the next 9 ingredients (jalapeños through cayenne pepper) and the remaining can of chilies. Rub this mixture all over the brisket and set the brisket into the crock. (If necessary, cut the brisket in half to fit into your slow cooker.) Cover and cook 9–10 hours on LOW (or 4–5 hours on HIGH).

3. Transfer the brisket to a platter and cover with foil to keep warm. Allow the brisket to rest for at least 10 minutes before cutting it into thin slices, against the grain.

4. While the meat rests, skim any visible fat from the surface of the vegetable mixture remaining in the crock. Stir in the lime juice.

5. To serve, arrange the meat slices on a platter and spoon the vegetables over the top or alongside. Garnish with cilantro, if desired.

2 (4.5-ounce) cans diced green chilies, divided

1 sweet onion, thinly sliced

1 red bell pepper, thinly sliced

½ cup ketchup

2 tablespoons quick-cooking tapioca

1 or 2 jalapeños, seeded and finely chopped

3 tablespoons kosher salt

2 tablespoons minced garlic

2 tablespoons lime zest

1 tablespoon ground chipotle pepper

1 tablespoon ground cumin

1 tablespoons sugar

1 tablespoon ground black pepper

½ teaspoon ground cayenne pepper or to taste

1 (5-pound) beef brisket, trimmed of visible fat

2 tablespoons fresh lime juice

¼ cup finely chopped fresh cilantro (optional)

Beef Tacos with Black Bean and Corn Salsa

Serves 6 (2 tacos each)

"Taco Night" is a favorite dinner at both of our homes. Leftover Chili and Lime Brisket (see page 163) makes a perfect taco filling. For a taco topping, we've gussied up store-bought salsa. Other than warming up the taco shells and reheating the meat, this meal requires no actual cooking, so how about delegating dinner to the kids?

For the salsa

1 cup store-bought salsa
   (such as Muir Glen®)

1 (15.5-ounce) can black beans,
   rinsed and drained

1 cup frozen corn, thawed

½ teaspoon cumin

⅓ cup thinly sliced scallions

1 tablespoon fresh lime juice

For the tacos

3 cups sliced brisket plus ½ cup cooking
   juices from Chili and Lime Brisket
   (see page 163)

12 store-bought taco shells (such as
   Ortega®)

2 cups shredded iceberg or romaine
   lettuce

1 avocado, chopped

1. Preheat the oven to 350°F.

2. Stir together the salsa ingredients in a bowl; set aside.

3. Add the brisket slices and cooking juice to a skillet over medium-low heat; cover and heat through, about 8 minutes.

4. Place the taco shells on a baking sheet; place in oven and turn off heat. This will crisp them up nicely without drying them out.

5. Assemble the taco ingredients in bowls to be served family-style. Each taco should have a bit of brisket, lettuce, avocado, and salsa.

Chinese Braised Brisket

Serves 8–12, depending on appetites

Beef brisket is both budget-friendly and slow cooker–friendly. Here we have seasoned it with heaps of ginger and garlic along with some traditional Chinese ingredients like sesame oil and five-spice powder. Kimberly always serves this meal with brown rice and steamed broccoli to sop up the aromatic sauce. Leftover brisket can be used in Spinach, Carrot, and Beef Noodle Bowls (page 166).

1. Stir together the first 7 ingredients (ginger through salt) in a large bowl. Rub the ginger mixture all over the brisket and set aside.

2. Stir together the onion, ketchup, tamari, tapioca, and vinegar in the slow cooker crock. Place the brisket on top. Sprinkling any remaining seasonings from the bowl over the top of the brisket. Cover and cook 9–10 hours on LOW (or 4–5 hours on HIGH).

3. Transfer the brisket to a platter and cover with foil. Allow the brisket to rest for at least 10 minutes before cutting it into thin slices, against the grain.

4. While the meat rests, skim and discard any visible fat from the surface of the onion mixture. Pour the cooking liquid and onion over the meat slices and serve.

3 tablespoons grated fresh ginger

3 tablespoons sugar

3 tablespoons minced garlic

2 teaspoons toasted sesame oil

2 teaspoons Chinese five-spice powder

1 teaspoon sriracha chili sauce (or regular hot sauce such as Frank's®)

¼ teaspoon kosher salt

1 (5-pound) beef brisket, trimmed of visible fat

1 onion, thinly sliced

¼ cup ketchup

⅓ cup wheat-free tamari (such as San-J®)

2 tablespoons quick-cooking tapioca

2 tablespoons rice vinegar

INGREDIENT INFO San-J® Tamari sauce is one of the best gluten-free soy sauce condiments that we have come across and we are pretty darn excited about it! Tamari lends a savory, salty kick to lots of foods—try it for yourself! For more information, check out the San-J website: www.san-j.com.

Spinach, Carrot, and Beef Noodle Bowls

Serves 4

½ pound rice vermicelli
(thin rice noodles)

boiling water

1 (32-ounce) package chicken broth
(such as Pacific Natural Foods®)

1 tablespoon grated ginger

1¼ teaspoon kosher salt, more to taste

1 teaspoon minced garlic

pinch ground black pepper

3 cups sliced Chinese Braised Brisket
with ½ cup cooking juices
(see page 165)

1 (5-ounce) package baby spinach

1⅓ cups julienne-cut carrots
(available in most supermarket
produce departments)

1 cup mung bean sprouts, rinsed

Garnishes

toasted sesame oil

thinly sliced scallions

wheat-free tamari sauce
(such as San-J®)

sriracha sauce

The key to successful noodle bowls is preparation—soaking the rice noodles, heating the broth, and assembling the garnishes so people can arrange their noodle bowls to their own liking. This preparation takes a bit of time, but none of it is difficult. This colorful dinner makes good use of leftover Chinese Braised Brisket (page 165). Wide and fairly deep bowls are the most appropriate for this noodle dish. And if you want to slurp your noodles, go ahead—that's how they're eaten at Asian noodle houses. At the end of this recipe, we've offered a list of vegetables that can also be used in these delicious noodle bowls.

1. Place the noodles in a 13 x 9-inch baking pan. Pour enough boiling water over the noodles to cover them with at least 1 inch of water. Allow the noodles to sit in the water for at least 10 minutes to soften. Stir them a few times to loosen them up.

2. Add the next 5 ingredients (broth through black pepper) and 4 cups of water to a soup pot over medium-high heat, and bring to a boil.

3. Warm the brisket in a skillet over medium heat (or in the microwave).

4. To assemble the bowls, divide the spinach between 4 bowls. Drain the noodles and divide them equally between the bowls. Add ⅓ cup of carrots and ¼ of the beef slices to each bowl. If incorporating any additional vegetables, do so before ladling 2 cups of broth into each bowl. Top each bowl with ¼ cup bean sprouts. Offer the garnishes family-style in the center of the table.

Additional Vegetables for Noodle Bowls

sautéed mushrooms and/or pepper strips

sautéed yellow summer squash or zucchini

steamed broccoli, green beans, or asparagus

watercress, pea shoots, snow peas, and/or thinly sliced radish

14
Sweets

Recipe Variation
DAIRY-FREE

Candied Pecans

Serves 14 (scant ¼ cup each)

This is a slow-cooked version of a classic, sweet pecan recipe. Try these as a garnish for chicken salad or add them to a homemade snack mix or your holiday dessert buffet.

⅔ cup sugar

½ teaspoon cinnamon

¼ teaspoon kosher salt

1 egg white

1 pound pecan halves

1. Whisk together the sugar, cinnamon, and salt in a medium bowl; set aside.

2. In a separate bowl, whisk the egg white until frothy. Add the pecans and stir until the nuts are well coated with the egg white. Transfer the pecans to the bowl with the sugar-cinnamon mixture and toss until they are evenly coated with the sugar.

3. Add the nuts to the slow cooker. Cover and cook 1 hour on HIGH. Stir the nuts, cover, and cook an additional hour.

4. Transfer the pecans to a baking sheet lined with parchment paper; allow them to cool completely. Transfer nuts to a serving bowl or store in a covered container at room temperature for up to 2 weeks.

DAIRY-FREE

Sweet Cardamom Walnuts

Serves 16 (¼ cup each)

These walnuts are the perfect addition to any holiday dessert buffet or cheese plate. The cardamom gives the nuts an interesting, slightly exotic flavor that's a nice change from typical sugared nuts.

1. Whisk together the sugar, cardamom, salt, and orange zest in a medium bowl; set aside.

2. In a separate bowl, whisk the egg white and vanilla until frothy. Add walnuts and stir until the walnuts are well coated with the egg white. Transfer walnuts to the bowl with the sugar-cardamom mixture and toss until they are evenly coated with the sugar.

3. Add the nuts to the slow cooker. Cover and cook 1 hour on HIGH. Stir the nuts, cover, and cook an additional hour.

4. Transfer the walnuts to a baking sheet lined with parchment paper; allow them to cool completely. Transfer nuts to a serving bowl or store in a covered container at room temperature for up to 2 weeks.

⅔ cup sugar

1½ teaspoons ground cardamom

⅛ teaspoon kosher salt

1 tablespoon firmly packed orange zest

1 egg white

½ teaspoon vanilla extract

1 pound walnut halves and pieces

NUTRITION NOTE A healthy addition to any diet, walnuts are packed with nutrients, primarily protein, fiber, and alpha-linolenic acid (ALA), the plant-based essential fatty acid.

Chocolate Bliss Fondue

Serves 15 (about ⅓ cup each)

Perfect for a party or Valentine's Day, this chocolate fondue will make you swoon. We suggest using chopsticks as fondue "forks" for dippers like fruit and marshmallows if little ones will be dipping, or if you don't happen to have fondue forks on hand.

1¼ cups light cream

1 cup heavy cream

¼ teaspoon vanilla extract

⅛ teaspoon instant espresso
   or instant coffee

pinch kosher salt

1 (24-ounce) bag semisweet
   chocolate chips

1. Stir together light cream, heavy cream, vanilla, espresso, and salt in the slow cooker crock. Cover and cook 30 minutes on HIGH.

2. Stir in chocolate. Cover and cook 30 minutes on HIGH. Whisk until mixture is smooth and evenly blended.

3. Reduce temperature to LOW for serving. Store any leftover fondue in the refrigerator. (We've never actually had any leftover fondue, but we suppose some people can exercise restraint!)

Suggested items for dipping

strawberries

banana slices

sliced kiwis

dried apricots

marshmallows (such as Campfire®)

gluten-free cookies

gluten-free pretzels

Dulce de Leche

Makes 3½ cups

This recipe is so easy it's hard to even call it a recipe. However, nobody has to know that! Having this amazing milk caramel on hand feels like a luxury, and we're sure you'll find myriad ways to use it. Kitty stirs it into coffee; it can also be spooned over vanilla ice cream or spread on apples or bananas. It also makes a lovely hostess or holiday gift.

1. Place the unopened cans into the slow cooker crock. Add enough hot water to reach ¾ of the way up the cans.

2. Cover and cook 6 hours on HIGH.

3. Carefully remove the cans and allow them to cool to room temperature, about 3 hours.

4. Open cans and scrape out the milk caramel. The caramel can be stored in the refrigerator for up to 1 month in a covered container.

2 (14-ounce) cans sweetened condensed milk, unopened, labels peeled off

water

DAIRY-FREE

Apricot, Cherry, and Pear Compote

Serves 12 (about ½ cup each)

This fragrant and colorful compote is delicious alone or served over Greek yogurt, cottage cheese, or hot cereal. It also makes a nice hostess gift.

2 ¼ cups hot water

1 ⅓ cups sugar

½ cup white wine

1 teaspoon orange zest or lemon zest

¼ teaspoon vanilla extract

pinch kosher salt

4 ripe pears (Bosc, Anjou, or Bartlett),
    peeled and cut into 1-inch pieces

1 ½ cups dried apricots

1 cup dried cherries
    (or dried cranberries)

1. Stir together the water, sugar, wine, zest, vanilla, and salt in the slow cooker crock until the sugar is dissolved. Add the pears, apricots, and cherries and stir well.

2. Cover and cook 6 hours on LOW (or 3 hours on HIGH). The pears should be tender and the dried fruit should be plumped. Serve warm or refrigerate to serve cold.

INGREDIENT INFO Floral wines, such as Moscato or Riesling, will work wonderfully in this recipe. If you shy away from cooking with wine, use ⅓ cup of apple juice plus 1 tablespoon lemon juice in place of the wine.

Vanilla Poached Pears

Serves 6

Poached pears, served warm or cold, are a delightful way to end a fall or winter dinner. To gussy them up a bit, serve the pears with whipped cream, ice cream, or lightly sweetened Greek yogurt. Reserve any poaching liquid for a flavorful addition to cocktails or iced tea, or mix it into hot cereals.

1. Stir together all ingredients except pears and mint in the slow cooker crock until sugar dissolves; set aside.

2. Peel, halve lengthwise, and core the pears. Add them to the crock and gently toss to coat them with the liquid. All pear halves should be mostly submerged in the poaching liquid.

3. Cover and cook 5–6 hours on LOW (or 2½–3 hours on HIGH). Pears should be fork-tender. Cool pears to room temperature, uncovered, in the poaching liquid. Discard vanilla bean. Transfer pears and poaching liquid to a container and refrigerate until needed.

4. Serve the pears cold or at room temperature. Garnish with mint and a bit of poaching liquid.

3 cups hot water

1½ cups sugar

3 tablespoons lemon juice

5 whole cloves (optional)

½ vanilla bean, split lengthwise to release seeds

1½ teaspoons vanilla extract

pinch kosher salt

6 fresh pears (Bosc, Anjou, or Bartlett)

fresh mint leaves (optional) for garnish

TECHNIQUE TIP A melon baller works famously for coring picture-perfect pears. If you don't have one, use a spoon to scoop out the seeds and pith.

Caramel Apple Crisp

Serves 4 (about 1½ cups each, including cookie topping)

This apple crisp is the perfect dessert to bring to a potluck or serve at a dinner party. You could certainly serve this dessert out of the crock, but we like serving it in a pretty baking dish.

¼ cup apple cider or apple juice

2 tablespoons cornstarch

5 Granny Smith apples, peeled and thickly sliced

2 tablespoons brown sugar

1 tablespoon butter

1 teaspoon lemon juice

¼ teaspoon ground cinnamon

pinch of kosher salt

⅓ cup store-bought caramel sauce (such as Mrs. Richardson's®)

6 small gluten-free oatmeal cookies (such as Glenny's®), crumbled

vanilla ice cream (optional) for topping

1. In a small bowl, whisk together the cider and cornstarch and add to the slow cooker crock. Add apples, sugar, butter, lemon juice, cinnamon, and salt to the crock and stir well. Cover and cook 3 hours on LOW (or 1½ hours on HIGH).

2. Stir gently and transfer the mixture to an 8-cup baking dish. Drizzle the caramel sauce over the apples and sprinkle the crumbled cookies over the caramel. Serve warm or at room temperature.

3. Top bowls with vanilla ice cream, if desired.

Cinnamon-Walnut Stuffed Apples

Serves 6

We love to serve these apples at fall dinner parties because they're delicious and special enough for guests. Plus, they're easily timed to be ready when you are: put them in the slow cooker just before the party starts and they'll be done just about the time your guests will be looking around for dessert. If you are fortunate enough to have any leftovers, refrigerate them and treat yourself to a decadent breakfast.

1. Add the cider and rum to the slow cooker crock; set aside.

2. Core the apples from the top, leaving the bottom intact so the stuffing doesn't fall out. For the best presentation, run a paring knife around the top of the cored apple to widen the cavity a bit, allowing more of the stuffing to show when the apples are filled.

3. Stir together the remaining ingredients (except the ice cream) in a medium bowl until well mixed. Spoon the filling into the cored apples. Carefully transfer the apples to the crock.

4. Cover and cook 3 hours on LOW (or 1½ hours on HIGH).

5. Serve each apple with a bit of the cooking juice spooned around it. Offer vanilla ice cream or a little heavy cream on the side, if desired.

¼ cup apple cider or apple juice

1½ teaspoons spiced rum or brandy (optional)

6 Golden Delicious apples

½ cup toasted, chopped walnuts

⅓ cup golden raisins

⅓ cup brown sugar

2 tablespoons melted butter

1½ teaspoons cinnamon

pinch kosher salt

vanilla ice cream or heavy cream (optional)

INGREDIENT INFO   Golden Delicious apples are a popular choice for cooking because they hold their shape well. Other varieties that are suitable for this recipe are Jonagold and Rome Beauty.

TECHNIQUE TIP   A melon baller is a very handy gadget for baked apples (and poached pears). It cuts cleanly into the apple, making coring easier and yielding a neater-looking cavity for stuffing.

Blueberry Clafoutis

Serves 6 generously (about ¾ cup each)

A classic French, country-style fruit dessert, clafoutis is a wonderful way to make use of sweet summer berries. The texture of clafoutis is interesting—rather like a pancake, but also custard-like. Serve it either for dessert or as a brunch-time treat.

1 teaspoon butter

½ cup gluten-free pancake mix
(such as Gluten-Free Bisquick®),
plus more for flouring the crock

1½ cups fresh blueberries
(or raspberries)

2 eggs

½ cup sugar

pinch kosher salt

⅔ cups milk

1¼ teaspoons vanilla extract

¼ teaspoon lemon zest (optional)

confectioner's sugar (optional)

1. Grease and flour the inside of the slow cooker crock with the butter and pancake mix. Sprinkle the berries over the bottom of the crock; set aside.

2. In a separate bowl, whisk together the eggs, sugar, pancake mix, and salt. Add the milk, vanilla, and zest, if using. Whisk until smooth. Pour the mixture over the berries.

3. Cover and cook 2½–3 hours on HIGH. The clafoutis will lightly brown around the edges and the center will set when it is done. (It will also be puffy when it is done cooking and deflate as it cools—this is normal.) Sprinkle confectioner's sugar over the top of the clafoutis, if desired.

INGREDIENT INFO We like the quality of Gluten-Free Bisquick® Pancake and Baking Mix; it is mildly flavored and works extremely well as a flour substitute in certain recipes.

Chocolate Drop Candies

Makes 16

Making candy doesn't get much easier than this! In fact, it's so easy and fun (and relatively fast) that we suggest you get some children involved. Our kids gobbled these up (okay, so did we), so we're pretty sure any kids you know will also approve. Feel free to vary the dried fruit and nuts to suit your taste.

1. Add milk chocolate and dark chocolate chips to the slow cooker crock. Cook 30–45 minutes on LOW, until chocolate is melted (stir with spoon to test, as the chips may not look melted). Stir to blend chocolates. Turn off slow cooker and unplug. Let chocolate sit in crock, undisturbed, for 5 minutes to cool slightly. Meanwhile, cover a large baking sheet with waxed paper; set aside.

2. Combine cereal, cherries, and pecans in a small mixing bowl. When chocolate has cooled slightly, stir the cereal mixture into the chocolate until well combined. Let mixture cool another 5 minutes; then add the marshmallows. Stir until all ingredients are coated with chocolate.

3. Drop mixture by heaping tablespoonfuls onto waxed-paper-lined baking sheet. Refrigerate 15–20 minutes, or until set. Store candies covered, at room temperature, for up to 3 days.

1 cup milk chocolate chips

¾ cup dark chocolate chips

¾ cup crisped rice cereal (such as Enjoy Life® Perky's Crunchy Rice Cereal)

½ cup dried cherries

½ cup chopped pecans

1 cup mini marshmallows

Classic Rice Pudding

Serves 6 (about ¾ cup each)

Kimberly loves nostalgic desserts like this classic rice pudding. She also loves that when you make pudding in a slow cooker, it is not likely to burn the way stove-top pudding tends to do.

2 cups hot water

1 cup long-grain white rice

1 (14-ounce) can sweetened condensed milk (regular or fat-free)

2 tablespoons butter

⅔ cup regular or golden raisins

1¾ cups milk, divided

1 egg, beaten

3 tablespoons sugar

¾ teaspoon ground cinnamon

⅛ teaspoon ground nutmeg (optional)

1 teaspoon vanilla extract

pinch kosher salt

1. Stir together the water, rice, condensed milk, and butter in the slow cooker crock. Cover and cook 2 hours on HIGH. Stir well. Cover and cook another 30 minutes on HIGH.

2. Add the raisins to the crock. In a separate bowl, whisk together 1 cup of the milk, the egg, sugar, cinnamon, nutmeg (if desired), vanilla, and kosher salt. Add the milk mixture to the crock and stir to combine. Cover and cook 1 hour on HIGH.

3. Turn off the heat and stir in the remaining ¾ cup milk. Allow pudding to sit uncovered for 30 minutes before serving. The pudding can be served warm, room temperature, or refrigerated and served cold later.

Coconut Rice Pudding

Serves 8 (about ¾ cup each)

With just a hint of ginger, nutmeg, and lime, this Caribbean-inspired pudding is a great make-ahead dessert. Look for dried coconut products in the natural foods aisle at your supermarket.

1. Stir together the first 11 ingredients (rice through nutmeg) in the slow cooker crock. Cover and cook 4 hours on LOW (or 2 hours on HIGH). Add the lime juice and stir well. Cover and cook another hour on LOW (or 30 minutes on HIGH). The rice should be tender and the pudding will be thick.

2. Turn off the heat and stir in milk. Allow the pudding to sit uncovered for 30 minutes before serving. The pudding can be served warm, room temperature, or refrigerated and served cold later. Add a bit more milk to thin the pudding, if desired.

3. Serve pudding topped with whipped cream and toasted coconut chips, if desired.

Dairy-Free Variation

Substitute coconut oil or canola oil for the butter. Use coconut milk in place of the regular milk.

1½ cups medium-grain brown rice

3¾ cups hot water

1 (14-ounce) can coconut milk (regular or light)

⅔ cup sugar

⅓ cup dried, unsweetened, shredded coconut

2 tablespoons butter

1 teaspoon vanilla extract

1 teaspoon fresh lime zest

⅛ teaspoon kosher salt

¼ teaspoon ground ginger

⅛ teaspoon ground nutmeg

2 teaspoons fresh lime juice

1 cup milk or more to achieve preferred consistency

whipped cream for topping (optional)

½ cup dried coconut chips, toasted, for garnish (optional)

INGREDIENT INFO Dried coconut chips are simply thick ribbons of coconut that make great garnishes. We typically buy ours at Whole Foods but other specialty stores may carry them. Toast coconut chips just as you would sliced almonds: a few minutes at low heat in a nonstick skillet will yield lovely, golden, toasted coconut.

Chocolate Risotto

Serves 10 (about ¾ cup each)

We've seen chocolate risotto served in fancy Italian restaurants and knew it would translate nicely to slow cooking. Impress your friends and family at your next dinner party with this unexpected chocolate treat. Leftovers keep beautifully in the refrigerator for several days if you'd rather keep it all for yourself!

1 cup arborio rice

2 cups hot water

1 (14-ounce) can sweetened condensed milk (regular or fat-free)

2 ½ cups milk, divided

¼ cup light brown sugar

1 tablespoon unsweetened cocoa

1 ½ teaspoons vanilla extract

⅛ teaspoon kosher salt

1 ½ cups semisweet chocolate chips

whipped cream for topping (optional)

fresh raspberries or strawberries for garnish (optional)

1. Stir together rice, water, and condensed milk in the slow cooker crock. Cover and cook 2 hours on HIGH. The rice should be tender and most of the liquid absorbed.

2. Add 1 cup of the milk, brown sugar, cocoa, vanilla, and salt. Stir until blended. Cover and cook 1 additional hour on HIGH.

3. Turn off heat and stir in the remaining 1½ cups milk and the chocolate chips. Let the pudding sit, uncovered, for 15 minutes. Stir again to combine all ingredients.

4. Transfer pudding to individual bowls and top each with whipped cream and fresh berries, if desired. (Pudding can also be refrigerated and either served cold or reheated in the microwave just before serving.)

Chocolate Raspberry Risotto

IN STEP 2: Substitute ⅓ cup seedless **raspberry jam** for the brown sugar and reduce the amount of vanilla to ½ teaspoon.

Mexican–Spiced Chocolate Risotto

IN STEP 2: Add ¼ teaspoon ground **chipotle pepper** and 1 teaspoon of ground **cinnamon**. If extra spice is desired, add a pinch of ground **cayenne pepper**.

Orange Chocolate Risotto

IN STEP 2: Substitute 2 tablespoons of **Grand Marnier** liqueur for the vanilla.

IN STEP 3: Stir in 1½ teaspoons fresh **orange zest** with the chocolate chips.

Almond and Amaranth Pudding

Serves 8 (about ½ cup each)

A staple grain of the Aztecs, amaranth is a tiny seed grain that can be prepared in both sweet and savory ways. Nutrition-wise, amaranth is high in fiber and contains calcium and iron. In this recipe, we balanced the "herby" qualities of amaranth with the sweetness of almond paste. Be sure to purchase pure almond paste, since marzipan (a specialty almond paste for molding) often contains wheat flour.

1 cup amaranth

2½ cups water

2 tablespoons butter

generous pinch of kosher salt

¾ cup milk

½ cup almond paste (such as Solo®)

⅓ cup sugar

2 eggs

1 teaspoon almond extract

½ teaspoon vanilla extract

½ cup sliced almonds, toasted

1. Stir together amaranth, water, butter, and salt in the slow cooker crock. Cover and cook 2 hours on HIGH.

2. While the amaranth cooks, use an immersion blender to combine the next 6 ingredients (milk through vanilla) in a bowl. Process until smooth; set aside. Alternatively, process these ingredients in a blender or a food processor.

3. Stir the almond paste mixture into the amaranth. Cover and cook another 30 minutes on HIGH. Let the pudding sit, uncovered, for 10 minutes. Serve the pudding warm or refrigerate until needed and serve cold. (The pudding will thicken as it cools.)

4. Before serving, garnish each portion with 1 tablespoon toasted almonds.

Strawberries and Cream

Top each portion with sliced **strawberries** and whipped **cream**; then garnish with **almonds**.

Oranges and Dates

IN STEP 3: Add 1½ teaspoons **orange zest** to the pudding.

Top each portion with sliced **dates** and thinly sliced fresh **mint leaves**; then garnish with **almonds**.

Pumpkin Pudding

Serves 6 (½ cup each)

A great make-ahead dessert for a gluten-free Thanksgiving dinner, this pumpkin pudding is even better when paired with whipped cream. Please note that given the custard-like nature of this dessert, the recipe isn't suitable for doubling.

Nonstick cooking spray

1 (15-ounce) can pumpkin puree (not pumpkin pie filling)

4 egg yolks, beaten

1¼ cup light cream

½ cup sugar

⅓ cup light brown sugar

1 teaspoon vanilla extract

¾ teaspoon cinnamon

¼ teaspoon freshly ground nutmeg or ⅛ teaspoon ground nutmeg

⅛ teaspoon ground ginger

pinch salt

whipped cream for topping (optional)

Candied Pecans for garnish (optional; see page 170)

1. Coat the bottom and sides of the slow cooker crock with cooking spray; set aside.

2. Whisk together remaining ingredients (except the optional whipped cream and pecans) in a large mixing bowl until smooth. Transfer mixture to the crock.

3. Cover and cook 4 hours on LOW (or 2 hours on HIGH). The pudding is done when the center is set and the sides are just lightly browned.

4. Before serving, whisk the pudding until smooth. Transfer the pudding to a large serving bowl or divide between individual bowls. Serve warm or refrigerate until needed. Serve with whipped cream and pecans for garnish, if desired.

15
Quick and Easy Sides for Slow Cooking

Recipe Variation
DAIRY-FREE

Cornbread Four Ways

Serves 8

Our cornbread is not exactly traditional, but we think you'll agree that it nicely fills the bread void. This moist and tender cornbread is a hit with both adults and kids, and we've offered a few different variations so you can tailor the recipe to suit the meal.

3 tablespoons melted butter, divided

2 eggs

½ cup milk

½ cup sour cream

3 tablespoons honey or maple syrup

1 cup cornmeal

¾ cup all-purpose gluten-free flour (such as Bob's Red Mill®)

1½ teaspoons baking powder

1½ teaspoons baking soda

¼ teaspoon kosher salt

1. Preheat the oven to 400°F. Use a pastry brush to generously grease an 8-inch baking pan (square or round) with some of the melted butter.

2. Whisk the remaining butter with eggs, milk, sour cream, and honey in a small mixing bowl; set aside.

3. In a separate mixing bowl, stir together the cornmeal, gluten-free flour, baking soda, baking powder, and salt.

4. Add the wet ingredients to the dry mixture, and stir just until combined (a few lumps are okay—do not overstir or the bread will become tough). Using a rubber spatula, scrape the batter into the buttered baking pan.

5. Bake for 18–22 minutes, until the top of the bread is golden and a cake tester comes out clean.

Bacon Jalapeño Cornbread

Add to the dry ingredients:

⅓ cup cooked **bacon** pieces
(such as Hormel®)
1 **jalapeño**, seeded and finely chopped,
more or less to taste

Parmesan Herb Cornbread

Add to the dry ingredients:

½ cup grated **Parmesan cheese**
1 teaspoon dried **Italian seasoning**

Scallion and Cheddar Cornbread

Add to the dry ingredients:

3 **scallions**, thinly sliced
¾ cup grated **cheddar cheese**

Classic Coleslaw

Serves 8 (about 1 cup each)

Raw vegetables are a delicious contrast to slow-cooked food, and this noncreamy coleslaw with classic flavors is a snap to throw together.

For the dressing

5 tablespoons cider vinegar

¼ cup olive oil

2 tablespoons sugar

½ teaspoon kosher salt

½ teaspoon celery seed

¼ teaspoon freshly ground black pepper

For the slaw

1 (1-pound) bag coleslaw mix

1. Stir together the dressing ingredients in a medium mixing bowl.

2. Add the coleslaw mix and toss well. Serve immediately or refrigerate for up to one day.

Sweet Dijon Slaw

Serves 6 (about ¾ cup each)

This cabbage slaw is a favorite in the Mayone kitchen, where it often shows up alongside a homey casserole like our Potato, Ham, and Leek Casserole (see page 132). The crunch of the cabbage and snappy dressing are a nice counterpoint to slow-cooked foods.

1. Whisk together the dressing ingredients in a medium mixing bowl until smooth.

2. Add the salad ingredients and toss well to coat with the dressing. Refrigerate until needed.

For the dressing

½ cup mayonnaise

3 tablespoons sugar

2 tablespoons Dijon mustard
(such as Grey Poupon®)

2 tablespoons cider vinegar

1¼ teaspoon celery salt

¼ teaspoon Tabasco®

For the slaw

1 (1-pound) bag of shredded
coleslaw mix

1 red or green bell pepper,
seeded and finely chopped

1 shallot, finely chopped

DAIRY-FREE

Asian Slaw

Serves 10 (about 1 cup each)

Colorful and crisp, this easy slaw is a perfect side dish for Cashew Chicken (see page 120). The make-ahead dressing saves you time. It is also delicious served over rice noodles.

For the dressing

⅓ cup rice vinegar

2 tablespoons peanut butter

2 tablespoons Bragg Liquid Aminos®

2 tablespoons sugar

1 tablespoon toasted sesame oil

1 teaspoon grated ginger

½ teaspoon minced garlic

¼ teaspoon kosher salt

pinch crushed red pepper

For the slaw

½ head Napa cabbage, core removed, thinly sliced (about 8 cups)

1 red bell pepper, cut into thin strips

2 cups julienne-cut carrots

4 scallions, thinly sliced

1. Stir together the dressing ingredients in a small bowl and set aside. (If making dressing ahead of time, transfer it to a lidded jar and refrigerate up to 5 days.)

2. To prepare the slaw, combine the vegetables in a large serving bowl. Add the dressing and toss well to coat the vegetables with the dressing. Serve immediately. Any leftovers will stay fresh in the refrigerator for one day.

DAIRY-FREE

Curried Broccoli Slaw with Raisins and Almonds

Serves 4 (about 1 cup each)

Precut broccoli slaw is a favorite staple in our kitchens. We love its practically endless possibilities. Pair this crunchy, flavorful salad with Garlic and Herb Roasted Turkey Breast (see page 126) or Creamy Butternut Pear Soup (page 64).

1. Whisk together the dressing ingredients in a medium mixing bowl (dressing will be thick).

2. Add the slaw ingredients and toss well to coat with the dressing. Refrigerate until needed.

For the dressing

¼ cup sour cream

¼ cup mayonnaise

1 tablespoon fresh lemon juice

1 teaspoon sugar

½ teaspoon curry powder

¼ teaspoon cumin

½ teaspoon kosher salt

pinch ground cayenne pepper
  or more to taste

For the slaw

1 (12-ounce) package broccoli slaw

1 scallion, thinly sliced

⅓ cup golden raisins

⅓ cup sliced almonds, toasted

Mixed Greens with Dates, Pine Nuts, and Gorgonzola

Serves 4

Simplicity is the key to this easy salad. Sweet dates, creamy gorgonzola, and crunchy pine nuts are tossed with spring greens and a classic vinaigrette. Serve it alongside Rosemary, Garlic, and Lemon Pork Roast (see page 140) for a complete meal.

For the dressing

¼ cup extra-virgin olive oil

2 tablespoons lemon juice

1 teaspoon red wine vinegar

¼ teaspoon kosher salt

⅛ teaspoon ground black pepper

For the salad

1 (5-ounce) package spring greens

⅓ cup crumbled Gorgonzola cheese

1 cup whole Medjool dates,
    pitted and quartered lengthwise

⅓ cup toasted pine nuts

pomegranate arils (seeds) (optional)

1. Whisk together the dressing ingredients in a small bowl until smooth. Alternatively, you can add the dressing ingredients to a lidded jar and shake to combine.

2. Layer the salad ingredients in a serving bowl or onto individual plates. Drizzle dressing over the top. Toss just before serving. Garnish with pomegranate arils, if using.

INGREDIENT INFO Medjool dates are very large, moist, sweet dates grown in Morocco, the United States, Jordan, and the Palestinian territories. If they are branded as "Medjool" and sold whole (sometimes organic), they are likely gluten-free. Sometimes they are repackaged in a facility that handles wheat-based ingredients, in which case they would no longer be gluten-free. As always, check the package label.

Barr's Green Beans Almondine

Serves 4

This recipe comes courtesy of Barr Hogen, a gifted chef and close friend of Kimberly's. We think her treatment of this classic side dish is quite inspired. Barr uses Marcona almonds and finishes the dish with lemon and a bit of fresh parsley. This side dish is a perfect complement to Apple and Thyme Roasted Chicken (see page 122) or Steak Diane Pot Roast (see page 153).

1. Trim the green beans and cut them into thirds on the diagonal; set aside.

2. Add the butter to a skillet over medium heat. When the butter is foamy and slightly browned, add the almonds. Cook and stir for about 1 minute (they'll smell wonderfully toasted). Transfer almonds to a bowl and toss them with the lemon zest.

3. Return the skillet to stove; add the ½ cup water and bring to a boil. Add the green beans, salt, and pepper. Cover and cook for about 5 minutes. Remove the lid and allow the water to evaporate over medium-high heat.

4. Remove from heat and add the almonds, parsley, and lemon juice. Toss together well and adjust seasonings, if necessary.

1 pound green beans, ends snapped

2 tablespoons butter

¼ cup Marcona almonds

1 teaspoon lemon zest

½ cup water

¼ teaspoon kosher salt or more to taste

⅛ teaspoon ground black pepper or more to taste

2 teaspoons finely chopped fresh parsley

2 teaspoons lemon juice

Dairy-Free Variation

Replace butter with olive oil; do not let it brown before toasting the almonds.

INGREDIENT INFO Marcona almonds are grown in Spain. They are flatter and rounder than common almonds and have a distinctive, toasted flavor. Typically they are roasted with olive oil and salt. Look for them in gourmet food stores or online. If you cannot find them, simply substitute slivered almonds.

Sautéed Zucchini with Grape Tomatoes and Balsamic Vinegar

Serves 4

Served hot or at room temperature, this vibrant vegetable side dish is a nice accompaniment to Bolognese Pot Roast (see page 152).

2 tablespoons extra-virgin olive oil

2 medium zucchinis, halved lengthwise and cut into ½-inch slices

1 teaspoon minced garlic

½ teaspoon kosher salt

⅛ teaspoon ground black pepper

¼ cup thinly sliced fresh basil

1 pint grape tomatoes, halved lengthwise

1½ teaspoons balsamic vinegar

3 tablespoons grated Parmesan cheese for garnish (optional)

1. Heat oil in a large skillet over medium heat. When hot, add the zucchini, garlic, salt, and pepper. Cook and stir until crisp-tender and just starting to brown, about 6–8 minutes.

2. Add basil, tomatoes, and balsamic vinegar and stir to combine. Garnish with Parmesan, if desired.

Dairy-Free Variation

Omit Parmesan garnish.

Asparagus with Brown Butter and Shallots

Serves 4

This easy, yet enticing side dish is a nice accompaniment to Steak Diane Pot Roast (see page 153).

1. Heat butter in a skillet over medium heat. When the butter is foamy and slightly browned, add the asparagus and shallot. Cook and stir for about 30 seconds until the asparagus and shallot are coated with the butter.

2. Add the water, salt, and pepper to the skillet. Cover and cook for about 5 minutes, until the asparagus is crisp-tender. Remove cover and cook until water is evaporated. Add the lemon juice and stir well. Serve immediately.

1 tablespoon butter

1 pound asparagus, ends trimmed, cut on the diagonal into 2-inch pieces

1 shallot, thinly sliced

¼ cup water

¼ teaspoon kosher salt

⅛ teaspoon ground black pepper

1 teaspoon fresh lemon juice

Dairy-Free Variation

Replace butter with olive oil, but do not heat it until brown. Instead, when the oil is hot, add the asparagus and shallot.

TECHNIQUE TIP The nutty flavor of brown butter can be a wonderful addition to both savory and sweet recipes alike. To make brown butter: heat butter over medium heat until it is foamy and gives off a pleasant, toasted aroma. Watch the butter carefully, since it doesn't take long for it to go from browned to burned! The length of time it takes to make brown butter depends on the amount of butter, the pan, and your stove.

Cauliflower Couscous

Serves 4 (¾ cup each)

Since we first developed a recipe for cauliflower "rice" in our *Big Book of Low-Carb* (Chronicle, 2005), we've decided it is more like couscous (without the gluten), making it perfect for Middle Eastern meals like Moroccan Chicken (page 116) and Lamb Tagine (page 74). Make it a point to double the recipe since it freezes well.

1 head cauliflower

3 tablespoons water

2 tablespoons butter

½ teaspoon kosher salt

⅛ teaspoon ground black pepper

1. Separate the cauliflower florets from the stems, and save stems for another purpose. Coarsely grate the florets in a food processor or by hand.

2. Add cauliflower and the remaining ingredients to a large skillet; stir well. Bring to a simmer over medium-high heat. Cover and cook for 5 minutes until most of the water has evaporated. Stir, and continue to cook until the cauliflower is tender, about 3 minutes more.

Dairy-Free Variation

Replace butter with olive oil.

INGREDIENT INFO Cauliflower is one of those versatile vegetables that most of us underutilize. Raw cauliflower is always suitable on a crudités platter and in salads, and it's also delicious roasted, mashed, and incorporated into soups.

GF Seasoning Salt

Makes about ⅓ cup

Store-bought seasoning salts have too many variables for safe gluten-free cooking. After a little trial and error, we developed a seasoning salt that can flavor anything from soup to nuts.

1. Combine all the ingredients in a jar. Cover and shake well. Spice mixture will keep for 3–6 months in a covered container in a cool, dry place.

DAIRY-FREE

¼ cup kosher salt

2 teaspoons onion powder

1½ teaspoons paprika

1 teaspoon ground black pepper

1 teaspoon garlic powder

½ teaspoon turmeric

GF Chili Powder

Makes about ½ cup

When following a gluten-free diet, spice blends can be a gray area. We prefer to play it safe and make our own. Our chili powder is a versatile spice blend that can be added to recipes or simply used on its own as a rub for meats, poultry, or seafood.

2 tablespoons paprika

2 tablespoons ground cumin

1 tablespoon plus 1 teaspoon
    garlic powder

1 tablespoon dried oregano

2 ¼ teaspoons ground chipotle pepper

1 ½ teaspoons kosher salt

1 teaspoon ground black pepper

½ teaspoon cayenne pepper,
    more or less to taste

1. Combine all the ingredients in a jar. Cover and shake well. Spice mixture will keep for 3–6 months in a covered container in a cool, dry place.

GF Barbecue Seasoning

Makes about ¼ cup

The formulation of commercial seasoning blends can change from time to time—without consumers knowing about it. If you are not in the habit of checking the ingredient label every time, you are not likely to notice if a gluten-containing ingredient found its way into the mixture. For seasoning mixtures that you use frequently, mixing up your own blend is an easy, safe way around this problem. This barbecue blend is a great rub for grilled meat and poultry, and it also adds zing to popcorn, nuts, sauces, or anything that needs a little spice!

1. Combine all ingredients in a jar. Cover and shake well. Spice mixture will keep for 3–6 months in a covered container in a cool, dry place.

2 tablespoons sugar

1½ teaspoons smoked paprika

¾ teaspoon ground ancho chile pepper

¾ teaspoon kosher salt

½ teaspoon onion powder

½ teaspoon garlic salt

¼ teaspoon dry mustard

¼ teaspoon black pepper

Resources for Gluten-Free Living

With the increased public attention to all things gluten-free, the number of resources available to consumers has quickly multiplied. New support and information networks, blogs, books, recipes, and experts seem to burst upon the gluten-free scene every day! Overall, that's a very good thing, because for the longest time there was a tremendous information vacuum about gluten-free living, which left many people feeling isolated and unsupported. The information bonanza about all things gluten-free, however, has made it difficult at times to tease out the best sources of information and advice. Here, we've attempted to provide a good selection of reputable organizations, manufacturers, books, magazines, blogs, websites, and other information resources to assist you and make it easier to find what you need. The list is not all-inclusive, but we hope it will be a good starting point to learn more about celiac disease and gluten-free living.

Celiac Organizations

AMERICAN CELIAC DISEASE ALLIANCE
Alexandria, VA
www.americanceliac.org

CELIAC DISEASE FOUNDATION
Studio City, CA
www.celiac.org

CELIAC SPRUE ASSOCIATION
Omaha, NE
www.csaceliacs.org

CANADIAN CELIAC ASSOCIATION
Mississauga, ON, Canada
www.celiac.ca

Consumer Information

CELIAC DISEASE AWARENESS CAMPAIGN
National Institute of Diabetes and Digestive
and Kidney Diseases
National Institutes of Health
Bethesda, MD
www.celiac.nih.gov

NATIONAL FOUNDATION FOR CELIAC
AWARENESS
Ambler, PA
www.celiaccentral.org

GLUTEN INTOLERANCE GROUP
OF NORTH AMERICA
Auburn, WA
www.gluten.net

CHILDREN'S DIGESTIVE HEALTH AND
NUTRITION FOUNDATION
Flourtown, PA
www.cdhnf.org

Blogs and Websites

BLOGS

www.befreeforme.com

www.beyondriceandtofu.com

www.beyondricecakes.com

www.celiacadvocate.com

www.celiacchicks.com

www.celiacteen.com

www.elanaspantry.com

http://glutenfreeblogcommunity.blogspot.com

http://glutenfreediet.ca/blog/

www.glutenfreeforgood.com/blog/

www.glutenfreefun.blogspot.com

www.glutenfreegirl.com

www.glutenfreehotproducts.com

www.gluten-freeliving.blogspot.com/

www.glutenfreeonashoestring.com

www.glutenfreeworks.com

www.surefoodsliving.com

www.wasabimon.com

www.thewholegang.org

WEBSITES

www.celiac.com

www.glutenfreeda.com

www.glutenfreerestaurants.org

www.kidswithfoodallergies.org

www.livingwithout.com

Magazines

Allergic Living
www.allergicliving.com

Delight Gluten Free Magazine
www.delightgfmagazine.com

Gluten-Free Living
www.glutenfreeliving.com

Living Without
www.livingwithout.com

A Few of Our Favorite Books on Celiac Disease and Living Gluten-Free

New books about food allergies, celiac disease, and gluten-free living and cooking are printed every year—it's a hot topic! We've listed some of our favorites below. Keep in mind that your local library likely has many appropriate books, too, in case you'd like to give a book a "test drive" first.

Celiac Disease Nutrition Guide
Tricia Thompson, MS, RD
American Dietetic Association
www.eatright.org

Gluten-Free Diet
Shelley Case, BSc, RD
Case Nutrition Consulting, Inc.
www.glutenfreediet.ca

Real Life With Celiac Disease
Melinda Dennis, MS, RD, LDN,
and Daniel A. Leffler, MD, MS
AGA Press
www.gastro.org/publications

Manufacturers of Slow Cookers

All-Clad (www.all-clad.com)

Cuisinart (www.cuisinart.com)

Farberware (www.farberware.com)

GE (General Electric) (www.gehousewares.com)

Hamilton Beach (www.hamiltonbeach.com)

KitchenAid (www.kitchenaid.com)

Presto (www.gopresto.com)

Proctor-Silex (www.proctor-silex.com)

Rival (www.crock-pot.com)

Toastmaster (www.toastmastercorp.com)

VitaClay (www.vitaclaychef.com)

West Bend (www.westbend.com)

About
the Authors

KIMBERLY MAYONE is a published cookbook author and owner of
WOW Delicious™, a company that works with clients, big and small, developing recipes to
their specifications. She is a regular contributor to *Fresh* magazine and has also written for
Health magazine; she is the editor of Flavorista.com. She lives in South Portland, Maine,
with her husband and three children.

KITTY BROIHIER, MS, RD, is a published cookbook author and owner
of NutriComm Inc., a food and nutrition communications consulting company serving
food companies and public relations firms. Previously on the editorial staff at *Good
Housekeeping* magazine, she has written many magazine articles and contributes regularly to
a variety of national and regional publications. She is a member of the American Dietetic
Association and currently serves as the president of the Maine Dietetic Association. She
and her children reside in South Portland, Maine.

Non-Liquid Ingredients
WEIGHTS OF COMMON INGREDIENTS IN GRAMS

INGREDIENT	1 CUP	¾ CUP	⅔ CUP	½ CUP	⅓ CUP	¼ CUP	2 TBSP
Sugar, granulated cane	200 g	150 g	130 g	100 g	65 g	50 g	25 g
Confectioner's sugar (cane)	100 g	75 g	70 g	50 g	35 g	25 g	13 g
Brown sugar, packed	180 g	135 g	120 g	90 g	60 g	45 g	23 g
Corn meal	160 g	120 g	100 g	80 g	50 g	40 g	20 g
Corn starch	120 g	90 g	80 g	60 g	40 g	30 g	15 g
Rice, uncooked	190 g	140 g	125 g	95 g	65 g	48 g	24 g
Couscous, uncooked	180 g	135 g	120 g	90 g	60 g	45 g	22 g
Table salt	300 g	230 g	200 g	150 g	100 g	75 g	40 g
Butter	240 g	180 g	160 g	120 g	80 g	60 g	30 g
Vegetable shortening	190 g	140 g	125 g	95 g	65 g	48 g	24 g
Chopped fruits and vegetables	150 g	110 g	100 g	75 g	50 g	40 g	20 g
Nuts, chopped	150 g	110 g	100 g	75 g	50 g	40 g	20 g
Nuts, ground	120 g	90 g	80 g	60 g	40 g	30 g	15 g
Parmesan cheese, grated	90 g	65 g	60 g	45 g	30 g	22 g	11 g

Note: Non-liquid ingredients specified in American recipes by volume (if more than about 2 tablespoons or 1 fluid ounce) can be converted to weight with the table above. If you need to convert an ingredient that isn't in this table, the safest thing to do is to measure it with a traditional measuring cup and then weigh the results with a metric scale. In a pinch, you can use the volume conversion table opposite.

Metric Conversions

Volume Conversions
NORMALLY USED FOR LIQUIDS ONLY

CUSTOMARY QUANTITY	METRIC EQUIVALENT
1 teaspoon	5 mL
1 tablespoon or ½ fluid ounce	15 mL
1 fluid ounce or ⅛ cup	30 mL
¼ cup or 2 fluid ounces	60 mL
⅓ cup	80 mL
½ cup or 4 fluid ounces	120 mL
⅔ cup	160 mL
¾ cup or 6 fluid ounces	180 mL
1 cup or 8 fluid ounces or half a pint	250 mL
1½ cups or 12 fluid ounces	350 mL
2 cups or 1 pint or 16 fluid ounces	475 mL
3 cups or 1½ pints	700 mL
4 cups or 2 pints or 1 quart	950 mL
4 quarts or 1 gallon	3.8 L

Note: In cases where higher precision is not justified, it may be convenient to round these conversions off as follows:

1 cup   = 250 mL
1 pint   = 500 mL
1 quart = 1 L
1 gallon = 4 L

Weight Conversions

CUSTOMARY QUANTITY	METRIC EQUIVALENT
1 ounce	28 g
4 ounces or ¼ pound	113 g
⅓ pound	150 g
8 ounces or ½ pound	230 g
⅔ pound	300 g
12 ounces or ¾ pound	340 g
1 pound or 16 ounces	450 g
2 pounds	900 g

Note: Ounces referred to in this table are not the same as fluid ounces.

Index

Note: Page numbers in **bold** indicate dairy-free recipes, and page numbers in *italics* indicate recipes that can easily be made dairy-free.

Recipe Index

Note: Page numbers in **bold** indicate dairy-free recipes, and page numbers in *italics* indicate recipes that can easily be made dairy-free.